Fight
Fundamen

C000170764

Fighting Fundamentalism

A Spiritual Autobiography

DOUGLAS BARTLES-SMITH

SAXTY PRESS

Published by Saxty Press
18 Vane Road, Shrewsbury, Shropshire sy3 7hb

© Douglas Bartles-Smith 2007

British Library Cataloguing in Publication Data
A catalogue record for this book is available from the British Library

ISBN 978–0–9555021–0–1

Designed and typeset by Bob Elliott
Printed by Hobbs the Printers Ltd, Totton, Hampshire

For Ann, Andrew, Sarah and Peter

FOREWORD

M Y hope is that this book will encourage others to fight against Fundamentalism which does so much harm in today's world. Christians need not fear the modern world and should not be very counter-cultural. We should follow Jesus in siding with the poor and the outcasts of society and in being inclusive of all people. In retirement I don't have to be diplomatic, so I have said what I really feel and believe.

I would like to thank Alan Heaton, the husband of my niece Julie, for typing the manuscript, and Archdeacon David Gerrard and Bishop Ronnie Bowlby for reading it and making helpful suggestions. Finally, it is appropriate that a member of the Lion Club, which is described in this book, is responsible for editing it. For this, my thanks go to Richard Hudson whose advice has been crucial.

DOUGLAS BARTLES-SMITH

Shrewsbury
January 2007

ACKNOWLEDGEMENTS

EVERY effort has been made to trace the copyright holders of all quoted material. Full details of sources are contained in the Notes at the end of the book. In particular the publishers are grateful to the copyright holders for permission to reproduce material from the following publications: *The Times*, the *Guardian*, the *Independent*, David Hare *Asking Around – Background to the David Hare Trilogy* (Faber & Faber and National Theatre 2003), Stephen Bates *A Church at War* (I. B. Taurus 2004), Trevor Beeson *The Bishops* (SCM Press 2002), *The Church Times*, A. N. Wilson *Against Religion – Counterblast 19* (Chatto and Windus 1991), Rowan Williams *The Body's Grace* (The Michael Harding Memorial Address, LGCM 2003), The South London Press, Kenneth Leech *The Sky is Red* (Darton, Longman & Todd 1997 & 2003), Esther Kaplan *With God on their Side* (The New Press, New York & London 2004 & 2005), Tariq Ali *The Clash of Fundamentalisms* (Verso New York 2002), *The Bridge* (Newspaper of the Anglican Diocese of Southwark), *The Salopian* No 136 June 2005 (Shrewsbury School), *The Church of England Newspaper*.

CONTENTS

CHAPTER 1

✺✝✺

Anglo-Catholic Childhood

T HE Church of England when I was a boy was very different from the Church today. In the 1930s Conservative Evangelicals had very little influence, but gradually, throughout my lifetime, this Militant Tendency within the church has grown in power and influence. Today they form the largest party in the Church and some of their number are close to returning the Church to a dark age of blinkered, bible-based bigotry.

My story is intertwined with their story. At the end we shall see the Archbishop of Canterbury and most other Bishops afraid to confront these extremists, and thereby failing to keep the Established church inclusive and available to all the people of England.

There is now a great need for religious leaders to challenge Religious Fundamentalism. The time for appeasement is over. Archbishop Desmond Tutu rightly sees Fundamentalism as a grave threat to world peace. 'Religious extremism filled the void created by the collapse of dictatorships and the end of the Cold War', he told diplomats at the United Nations, 'That is when Fundamentalisms arise, because then people are deeply distressed by complexity,' he explained. 'They look for simplistic answers.'[1]

This is happening within Christianity as well as Islam. President Bush is a Born Again Christian and was elected largely because of the Conservative Evangelical vote in the United States. At the end of this book I shall argue that there is as much need for Christian leaders to challenge Fundamentalism within Christianity as there is for Muslim leaders to do so within Islam.

Fundamentalists find their 'authority' solely in the literal inerrancy of scripture, which is the Word of God. But Anglicans must find 'authority' not only in 'scripture', rightly interpreted, but also in 'tradition', meaning the whole inspired experience of the Church of Christ, and in 'reason' as the God-given glory of humanity. All these are necessary to find the truth. Fundamentalists rely only on one, and the lack of any real 'authority' being given to 'reason' is a sign of both Christian and Muslim Fundamentalism.

My first sermon delivered when I was five years old was perhaps prophetic as it upset my mother's Conservative Evangelical relatives. It was my custom to play at celebrating Mass with my brother Allan acting as server. At Christmas a sermon was included and was listened to by the whole family as well as by mother's Fundamentalist relatives. My message was that Jesus was born in a pub. This greatly amused the Anglo-Catholic members of the family, but not the Evangelical relatives. This was my first encounter with Religious Fundamentalism.

My playing church showed how much the High Mass at St Mary's Shrewsbury grasped me from an early age. It is a large and beautiful church full of fine medieval stained glass and dating back to Saxon times. The Sung Eucharist was then accompanied by an excellent choir and I was captivated by the musical settings and the mystery of the Mass. I gradually understood that we were present to meet the Lord in the Sacrament of the Altar rather than listen to the sermon. My father made this very clear by pretending to go to sleep during the sermon. But nevertheless at family lunch afterwards he would tear it to pieces. The message always was that the sermon had to be endured so we were there for the moment when Christ was really present in the Sacrament of the Altar.

The Mass over, the men in the congregation went down to the Lion Hotel for a pre-lunch drink with the clergy and choir. For Jesus to be born in a pub was therefore very appropriate. To Catholics like us the Mass and the pub went together.

My father, however, had not been brought up as an Anglo-Catholic. He was in fact discouraged from going to church by his mother Annie Bartles. For the Bartles side of the family were very secular and early feminists. My grandfather who became postmaster at Ross-on-Wye would like to have gone to church but was not bold enough to do so until after his wife died.

My father used to visit his grandfather Ebenezer Norville Smith for holidays at Beachy Head near Eastbourne in Sussex. He was a telegraphist who looked after the telephone cable which went from there to France. He was a warm and religious person whom my father loved more than his own parents, so he came under a Catholic influence and was aware that Gramp, as he was called, used to go to Eastbourne to drink with the Anglo-Catholic Vicar.

But the converting moment for my father came not at Eastbourne but in Birmingham where he was brought up and went to school. He had a friend who sang in the choir at St Alban Highgate. He used to wait for him outside the church until one day a priest spotted him and dragged him into church. Father talked about this priest with awe. He had come from Northern Ireland where the Conservative Evangelicals were in control. These were the people who produced the Reverend Ian Paisley and were fanatically opposed to Catholicism. The Church of Ireland was more low church than Evangelical, but Anglo-Catholicism was not tolerated, and father's priest had not been allowed to perform the full Catholic rites. Even his family were not prepared to put up with what they saw as popery. So he came to Birmingham which as we shall see was not free of such bigotry but where he was able to perform the Catholic rites.

What most appealed to father as a young teenager was the way the Irish priest dealt with young people. He had been known to hitch up his cassock and fight with his fists when threatened by a teenage gang who quickly learnt that it was unwise to provoke him.

Father was soon prepared for Confirmation and confirmed by Bishop Gore, then Bishop of Birmingham. He always remembered the actual moment of the laying on of hands which he said was like an electric shock. His parents of course did not attend. Gore noticed this and singled father out for special attention. He subsequently always greatly admired Bishop Gore and read Gore's famous book *Lux Mundi* which was always prominently displayed in our house.

I am not sure my father realised how radical was the book edited by Gore. It was the *Honest to God* of the time. In it Gore argued that the results of Old Testament criticism must be accepted and the humanity of Christ must be recognised. 'Jesus', he wrote, 'never exhibits the omniscience of bare Godhead in the realm of natural knowledge; such as would be required to anticipate the results of modern science and criticism. Indeed God declares his almighty power in his condescension, whereby he "beggared" himself of Divine prerogatives to put himself in our place.'[2] In other words the Incarnation was a real Incarnation. Jesus was limited as a human being to the thought forms and knowledge of his own day. This came to be known as the Kenotic (self-emptying) theory of the Incarnation.

Gore's socialism never got mentioned at home, perhaps because my father always voted Conservative. The Community of the Resurrection which Gore founded was, however, greatly admired. Whenever a Mirfield Father came to Shrewsbury we always went to hear him and he often dined or stayed with the family.

Meanwhile in Birmingham my father began his life-long commitment to Anglo-Catholicism. This was not easy as some Conservative Evangelicals in Birmingham objected to the Mass being celebrated in the Church of England. The protests sometimes took an ugly form. My father described to us children how the Evangelicals went up into the gallery of the church to make a noisy protest whilst the Mass was in progress. Nevertheless the brave Anglo-Catholics below continued with incense and bells to obey our Lord's command to celebrate Mass. This made a big impression on me as a young boy and I was proud to identify myself with these brave Catholics.

My father eventually went to Birmingham University and qualified as a dental surgeon. He married Ellen Bonner in 1915 and moved to Shrewsbury in 1918 to start up a dental practice. In the early 1920s he changed his surname from Smith to Bartles-Smith. He was already Leslie Charles Bartles Smith. He merely added the hyphen. There was another dentist in the town called Smith who had been involved in a scandal and father wanted to make it clear it was not him.

His first wife died in 1934 leaving him with two young girls. Cynthia and Marion had been born in 1923 and 1925. From 1934 they were both looked after by their secular grandmother. She was then aged 70 but still determined to do her duty. Father would rush home after work to make sure his daughters said their prayers as he knew his mother would never do so.

In 1936 father married Muriel Rose Saxty. She was then his nurse in the dental surgery. At the age of 22 she became stepmother to two young girls. In 1937 I was born, followed by my brother Allan in 1939 and my sister Susan in 1945. My mother was a Methodist, and only became Anglo-Catholic when she married. The Evangelical relatives were on her mother Jane Cartwright's side of the family. Her father John Saxty was a clerk with the Great Western Railway but he died young, and so it was the mostly Baptist Cartwrights who had the greater influence. One result was that mother never drank alcohol till she met my father. The first time he took her out for a meal with friends she discovered what one glass of wine will do especially if you are not used to it. From then on mother was always encouraged to have a glass!

We lived in the centre of Shrewsbury, at 10 College Hill, in a large four storey Georgian house. The ground floor was the surgery and patient's waiting room. The family lived in the storeys above. There was a large garden where we played. The arrangement was not ideal for us children, for whenever there were no patients in the surgery, father was apt to do us a favour by examining our teeth to make sure they were in good order. This meant that we scanned the appointment book for gaps, and then made sure we were out. However, father nearly always managed to get us into his dental chair once during the holiday. My brother has hardly visited a dentist since then.

We both went to the only Anglo-Catholic prep school in Shrewsbury. Prestfelde School was chosen for this reason. We were very happy there, but it was academically very weak. Now it is a very good school. Father Dovey and Father Young were the headmasters in my day. Father Rice was the Chaplain and prepared me for Confirmation. I made my first confession in the school chapel when twelve years old. I was a very pious young boy in those days and had felt called to the priesthood from a very early age.

There was a lot of support from the family and from Father Mackenzie, the Vicar of St Mary's. Father would have liked to be a priest himself but felt he was not good enough. He may have been right for he had quite a temper at times and he frequently argued with Father MacKenzie. He did not suffer fools gladly and might have found it difficult to be pastoral with some people. He was, however, a Church-warden for many years and was strongly in favour of the disestablishment of the Church of England, something I never agreed with him about. He had been heavily involved in the Prayer Book controversy in the 1920s when Parliament failed to approve the new more Catholic Prayer Book. It did not stop the new Prayer Book being used at St Mary's Shrewsbury, but it made my father and many others determined to bring about disestablishment if they could.

The Catholicism of the 1950s was very different from the divided and sometimes strident Catholicism in the Church of England today. It was confident, moderate and liberal in its approach. I felt very much at home at High Mass in St Mary's, and my education at Prestfelde was support-ive of an intelligent Christianity, which was also preached by Mirfield Fathers when they came to Shrewsbury.

I was already aware, however, of another expression of Christianity which was far from intelligent. My Evangelical relatives had not been idle. This was the time when Evangelicalism was beginning to revive and my relatives always tried to get my mother, sister Cynthia and myself to attend their Baptist church when a star Conservative Evangelical came to preach.

And so it was that I heard the Evangelical sermon for the first time. I say Evangelical sermon because it was always essentially the same thought dressed up in different trappings. It was a sermon which even as a boy I greatly disliked. How could God be such a monster as to will the violent death of his own son so that sin could be taken away?

Steve Chalke, a prominent Baptist minister, whom I got to know later in life, puts it well in his recent book *The Lost Message of Jesus.*

The fact is that the Cross isn't a form of cosmic child abuse – a vengeful father, punishing his son for an offence he has not even committed. Understandably, both people inside and outside of the Church have found this twisted version of events morally dubious and a huge barrier to faith.[3]

However my father who disapproved of us hearing Evangelical preachers organised his own revenge. He would arrange for my Conservative Evangelical relatives to be invited to tea to be followed by a church service. He would make sure it was a feast day of Our Lady when the ritual and hymns were especially trying for Evangelicals to endure. We then had great fun watching closely to see how our relatives responded when we all began to sing, 'Hail Mary, Hail Mary, Hail Mary full of Grace!'

At the time I thought my father sometimes went too far. For in the 1950s Conservative Evangelicals were no real threat to the Church of England. Bishop Colin Buchanan, with whom I later worked when he was Bishop of Woolwich, makes this very clear in his book *Is the Church of England Biblical?* 'There was a "backs to the wall" persecution complex', he wrote. 'No Evangelical ever became a Bishop; the Evangelical colleges and their whole theological stance were dubbed "stone age" by the rest of the Church.'[4]

In 1956 Colin went to see his old head teacher and revealed that he was now an Evangelical. The head teacher's response was, 'I prefer something more intellectual myself.'[5] My father and many others would have agreed, and could not have envisaged a time when Conservative Evangelicals with their 'stone age' theology would come to dominate the Church. So perhaps father was right to warn of the danger.

❧✠❧

CHAPTER 2

A Questioning Education

IN 1950 I went to Shrewsbury School which was academically much better than Prestfelde but not Anglo-Catholic. I was a day-boy and my housemaster Stacy Coleman told me I had been held back by the teaching at Prestfelde, so I started in the bottom form, but soon began to respond to the better quality of teaching. Stacy was a surprisingly good housemaster of the dayboys. He was the last great classical Master of the Upper Sixth, whose students excelled at Oxford and Cambridge; but he also devoted himself, as housemaster, to those of lesser abilities. In his later years he became a Reader at St Mary's Shrewsbury where he preached regularly. He was aware of the strong links between St Mary's and the School, where the boys had worshipped for nearly 300 years, and where the School still worships once a year. Some remember that in 1855 four boys from the School climbed the 220 foot spire of St Mary's led by a future clergyman, J. A. Warren, whose account of the incident is in the school library.

For the first time I attended the service of Mattins which was compulsory for dayboys, even on a Sunday. In more recent years I have come to appreciate Mattins but the compulsory service at Shrewsbury put me off for years. The churchmanship at school was Central and was typical of what the Church of England had been for most of the century. It is extraordinary that this Central churchmanship which used to dominate the Church of England is today so very weak.

Mattins and Evensong were the compulsory services, but Shrewsbury did also acknowledge in a minor way the existence of Anglo-Catholics and Evangelicals. For the Catholics there was an occasional and voluntary sung Eucharist which I attended. It did not begin to compare with St Mary's and was done in a very low church way. Colin Lowry and I were the only boys to genuflect during the Creed to honour the Incarnation. This was one of the signs of a true Anglo-Catholic in those days.

For Evangelicals there was Michael Tupper, one of the chaplains. I was very careful not to go to any of his groups or holiday camps. Nevertheless

I was aware through him and my Evangelical relations that Billy Graham was in the country in 1954–1955. My sister Cynthia went to one of his rallies and was greatly impressed. This was the beginning of an Evangelical revival which was to change the Church of England almost beyond recognition by the time I retired.

I enjoyed life at Shrewsbury School even though it was still the era of the old-style public school. In other words beating and douling (the Shrewsbury term for fagging) still continued. I was a doul and ran errands for senior boys and was beaten as most boys were in those days. When I became head of house and a praeposter (school monitor) boys were beaten by me and the other monitors, and douls fagged for us. That was how it was in the 1950s. Looking back, the thing I disliked most was the way notices were given out. A doul would stand on a table and give out the notice and say, 'God Save the Queen and down with the radicals'! Later, whilst still at Shrewsbury, I would see the radicals as the real heroes.

I also learnt to enjoy cross-country running. There was a moment I remember on a school run when instead of ceasing to run hard when it became painful, I continued and went through the pain barrier, and so became a cross-country runner. I trained every day and eventually won both junior and senior steeplechases.

Shrewsbury had an organised system of cross-country running earlier than any other school. The Royal Shrewsbury School Hunt controlled running and consisted of huntsman, senior and junior whips and gentlemen of the runs (school colours). The hounds were the boys who raced. I was eventually junior whip and dressed up with cap, hunting horn and whip. My job was to see that no runner was behind me. The huntsman, similarly dressed up, was at the front and set the pace. The first part of the hunt was non-competitive, but the last two miles or so was a race for the hounds. The huntsman, whips and gentlemen went ahead and encouraged the hounds towards the end of the race. The first hound home killed (won) and then might become a gentlemen of the runs himself. It was all great fun and had nothing to do with foxes or real hounds. I also ran the half-mile in athletics, gaining my school colours when coming first against Repton and Malvern. Michael Charlesworth was the Master in charge of athletics, and he encouraged me to become the fastest half-miler the school had discovered for some years. Today the school has abandoned athletics, which I find an extraordinary decision, with the London Olympics now arranged for 2012. However, the Hunt still flourishes.

After two years I chose to go onto the classical side and was taught by two future headmasters. Antony Chenevix-Trench who became headmaster of Eton and Fettes School in Scotland, and Michael Hoban who became headmaster of Harrow. After a year I moved to the history side and was taught by Michael Charlesworth in the Lower Sixth and by Laurence Le Quesne in the Upper Sixth.

It was an exciting time to be at Shrewsbury. My exact contemporaries were Richard Ingrams, Paul Foot, William Rushton and Richard Booker. John Ravenscroft (John Peel) was also there but our paths did not cross. Laurence Le Quesne, a young censor of *The Salopian* (the school magazine) was encouraging the future founders of *Private Eye* to produce material for *The Salopian*. It was similar to what they later produced for *Private Eye*. Some of Rushton's cartoons were as good as many he did later.

Laurence Le Quesne was mildly left wing and encouraged questioning. He had an amazing laugh which greatly encouraged us all. William Rushton said years later, 'He was the reason I pursued comedy . . . Le Quesne laughed at every joke with the loudest laugh you'd ever heard.'[1]

The four of them were very different. Paul Foot and Richard Booker were both liberals and interested in politics. They were asking important questions which I was also asking. Richard Ingrams never stood for anything and made fun of everything. He divided people into pseuds and bores. Pseud was a term he invented. There was a pseud's tie worn by the editorial team and those approved of by Ingrams. Rushton was very likeable and funny but not religious or ambitious and rather lazy. He never got to university which was quite a difficult feat for anybody at Shrewsbury in those days.

Frank McEachran (Kek) was another teacher with a great influence. Every lesson he took involved each boy in the class standing on a chair and reciting by heart poetry, which had been broken down into short memorable extracts. These were called 'spells' and reflected the music of poetry. Many Salopians never forgot them and continue to recite them today.

An example might be this passage from Auden and Isherwood's play *The Ascent of F6*

At last the secret is out, as it always must come in the end,
The delicious story is ripe to tell to the intimate friend;
Over the tea-cups in the square the tongue has its desire;
Still waters run deep, my dear, there's never smoke without fire.[2]

It was not the best way to pass English A Level but it was a real education which boys remembered and benefited from for the rest of their lives.

Such a radical Shrewsbury was a challenge to faith. It was a very questioning environment which satirised all institutions, including the Church. I still believed in God and argued strongly for the Catholic faith with my fellow sixth formers and with Laurence Le Quesne. But Shrewsbury was changing me and I was becoming more liberal in politics and religion. I could no longer believe certain parts of the Bible and for the first time was beginning to question whether I ought to be ordained.

Guy Furnival the school chaplain was very helpful at this time. A group of us including Paul Foot met with him to discuss matters of faith and he introduced me to Bishop Gore's *Reconstruction of Belief.* This put together three of Gore's previous books on God, Christ and the Church. It did not answer all my queries but represented a real attempt to meet the intellectual challenges of the day and explain Christianity. The fact that Gore's book, written in the 1920s was still the best available in the 1950s, spoke volumes about the conservative nature of the church before the 1960s. There was a theology available which could have answered my queries but this was deliberately kept from most clergy and lay people at that time. It would not be until theological college several years later that I read Bultmann, Tillich and Bonhoeffer.

Meanwhile the study of history excited me greatly. Laurence Le Quesne was a brilliant teacher and also a Christian. Indeed when he first came to Shrewsbury he went to the same Baptist church as my Evangelical relatives. He taught in the Sunday School for a time and in those days did not drink alcohol. Peter Knight, another teacher at the school, told me he brought about Laurence's Conversion to the delights of good conversation and a pint of beer. He then joined the Lion Club which had been started by Kek in the 1930s. Kek, Peter, Laurence, Cyril Hayward-Jones (a blind teacher in town) and others would meet weekly in the Lion Hotel for serious and erudite discussion over pints of beer. After I left school I would often join them, as I would do later in life when on holiday with the family in Shrewsbury. Although Kek died in 1976, the club is still going strong today.

Kek was as well known in the Town as he was at the Lion Hotel and the school. He was often seen in cafes drinking coffee and reading a book, which he was happy to discuss with people he knew. Kek also read theology, and I once found him reading Professor C. H. Dodd's commentary on The Epistle of Paul to the Romans, which he greatly admired. He taught girls at other local schools who also recited his 'spells'. He enjoyed Scottish dancing, and I sometimes attended the classes which he organised during the school holidays for boys and girls from the town, held at the Priory Girls School. Kek was the happiest bachelor I have ever known, though he could get very angry with a few boys who did not cooperate with his style of teaching.

Peter Knight also taught me English. However he rarely arrived on time especially when it was the first lesson of the day at 7.45 a.m. before breakfast. On one occasion he famously met the headmaster Jack Peterson on the way to class. Jack Peterson said, 'Late again Mr Knight!' and Peter replied, 'So am I, Headmaster'!

Laurence Le Quesne eventually became an Anglican and went to St Chad's Shrewsbury. He greatly encouraged me to question and be radical in politics and religion. Indeed our discussions which began in 1955 have continued down the years and are still ongoing. I learnt from him to seek for the truth fearlessly and never stop asking questions. It was very important to me then that a person like Laurence still believed Christianity and went to church. This contrasted with others like Willie Rushton who refused to take religion seriously. Hence his comment when asked about religion, 'Good heavens no, I was spared that'![3]

Shrewsbury also opened my eyes to poverty in the inner cities. The school ran a mission in Everton, Liverpool, called Shrewsbury House. Boys from the school would go there most weeks for a weekend. Shrewsbury House boys would also visit the school site for football and swimming fixtures. In the summer they would camp at the school for two weeks. I was involved in all these activities, and for the first time had conversations with people from an entirely different background. I began to see what an inner city environment was like. This was to have a profound effect, and I started to be very critical of the government which did little to close the gap between rich and poor. Michael Heseltine was another Shrewsbury boy who was influenced by the School Mission, and who later as a Minister in the Conservative government did a lot for Liverpool.

Michael Heseltine came back to Shrewsbury after he left with another old Salopian Julian Critchley to debate a motion at the School Debating Society. It was to be a famous occasion. They won a debate on the motion 'that this house deplores the Public School system' against the future headmaster of Eton (Tony Chenevix-Trench) and of Harrow (Michael Hoban) who taught me classics. I voted for the motion. The result was leaked to the Press who reported that Public School boys had voted to abolish their school. It was not quite like that, but Michael Heseltine and Julian Critchley were not very popular with the school authorities for a time. Of course things changed after they both became famous.

In the holidays I often watched Shrewsbury Town play at the Gay Meadow. My brother Allan and I have watched them since we were eight years old. We saw them become champions of the Midland League and still remember the bald figure of their central defender and captain, Steve Hughes. I watched them beat Wrexham in their first ever home Football League game. I saw Arthur Rowley score many goals for the Town, including one which set the record for the number of league goals scored. When I lived in London I watched them at away games and have seen them beat Chelsea, West Ham, Crystal Palace and Millwall. Unlike my brother, who now supports Manchester United, I have remained loyal and still support them today. Many people who have known me over the years automatically think of me when they hear the Shrewsbury Town result.

Before leaving Shrewsbury I accepted a place to read history at St Edmund Hall, Oxford, but they required me to do National Service first. Shrewsbury had encouraged me to be radical and ask questions. Christopher MacLehose, who was in the sixth form with me and became head of Harvill Press, put it more sharply when he told Humphrey Carpenter, 'People were encouraged at Shrewsbury to be pretty insolent'[4]. We all benefited from this open culture which allowed us to be creative, including the future writers of *Private Eye*, even if they did not always acknowledge it.

CHAPTER 3

※✝❧

The Army Fosters Ordination

I T was difficult to leave Shrewsbury School where I had been very happy as Head of House and a praeposter (school monitor) to undergo the discipline of basic training at Shrewsbury barracks. Laurence Le Quesne was very supportive and wrote me an encouraging letter which I have since used in sermons particularly when leaving a job.

As for the waters of Babylon, Sion wouldn't be Sion if one didn't leave it. I am sure that's true – it's why I left myself. If you enjoy things enough, the only thing to do, the only way to avoid ruining them is to give them up. You'll find that stated innumerable times in all sorts of ways in the New Testament (and elsewhere), e.g. the corn of wheat which has to die. Things are made to be burnt up. The faster you throw things away, the faster you find more coming to you and everybody else is better off; the fatal thing is to try to hold on to what you already have, instead of passing it on and looking for something else. What I spent, I had; what I gave, I kept; what I saved, I lost – one of the best epitaphs ever written. Only of course it's a long term thing. It's good to leave Sion if both Sion and yourself are not to grow stale, but that doesn't mean that grief isn't real. It must be. The weeks are long and dreary, but splendour of God! (as William the Conqueror used to say), you get your money for it in the end.

It was a difficult time at first. I was then close to being a pacifist and questioned on moral grounds whether I should be in the army at all. I realised, however, that I was not certain enough to go before a board to seek exemption. Basic training had hardly begun before the Suez Crisis suddenly erupted. I was certain the war was wrong. I was a *Guardian* reader at the time and agreed wholeheartedly with the newspaper's opposition to the war. Luckily, the crisis was over before I finished basic training and I was therefore never faced with the prospect of taking part.

Basic training brought me into contact with people from a different background. Paul Foot was with me again, but most were working-class young men away from home for the first time. I learned more about the needs people have, particularly the need to find some meaning in life. I believed William Blake was right to say that 'man is either the ark of God or a phantom of earth and water.' James Joyce points in Ulysses to the only real alternative to belief in God, and that is complete and utter despair. Joyce looks beyond this world to the dark void when faith once beheld light. He looks upon the void and he dares to bring into conscious expression the fear which lies deep in the soul of modern people: the fear that the glory of humans is utterly meaningless. Joyce of course was an atheist; but he was an honest atheist. Once Christianity was rejected he was not afraid to spell out the only logical alternative. In the army I saw very clearly how much people needed a meaning in their lives, and I wanted to help them find it. As a result I once again became certain that God was calling me to be ordained to the priesthood. I began therefore to take the necessary steps to have my vocation tested by the Church.

My generation was taught to kneel down by our beds to say prayers. Today of course it is different and people adopt a number of positions for prayer. But in 1956 a committed Christian knew his duty. He should be ready to kneel down by his bed in front of all the other soldiers in the barrack room. I had been dreading this moment and was afraid I would not have the courage to do it. However the courage was there and I knelt down by my bed and was very grateful when no-one mocked me. I was the only person in the barrack room to kneel down and say prayers.

We did not see a great deal of the officer in charge of basic training. He was Captain Simon Raven who became a distinguished novelist. He was later allowed to leave the army in a gentlemanly fashion when he got himself into debt. We did not see much of him, because the Commandant of Shrewsbury barracks believed that the social obligations of regular officers in their own county, like Simon, took precedence over mundane military chores like recruit training, which could be safely undertaken by non-commissioned offers and National Service Officers.[1]

Simon himself wrote, 'In summer one was expected to turn out for the Depot or the Shropshire Gents two or three times a week. That was no hardship. In winter those of us who were able hunted, while the rest of us did our share of rough shooting.'[2] This clearly suited Simon, and when he did meet us, he persuaded a fellow ordinand friend of mine to write his weekly Spectator article for him.

For a short time I was a member of the Intelligence Corps. My main memory is of taking part in surveillance training exercises at Lewes in Sussex. I would begin early in the morning sitting in a café drinking coffee reading a particular newspaper. Someone would enter whose job it was to tail me for the rest of the day. I would let him follow me for about ten minutes. Then I would hop on a bus and quickly lose the person who was tailing me. The rest of the day was then mine.

I eventually enjoyed army life. At first it made one appreciate normal life more, one's home, books and freedom. But in the end it was very much more than this, especially when one became an officer. I was chosen to command the passing out parade for those of us being commissioned. For two weeks I worked closely with the sergeant-major to rehearse the parade and my own sword drill. I came to enjoy and appreciate the intricacies of drill and the joy and beauty of getting it right.

I was commissioned as a Second Lieutenant in the Royal Army Service Corps and was sent to Maryhill Barracks in Glasgow. I had been hoping to be sent abroad. My parents, however, had other ideas, and were praying this would not happen. They especially did not want me to go to Cyprus or Kenya where fighting was taking place. So I went to Glasgow. This sometimes felt like abroad and was certainly then very grim. Drunks at night were very obvious and numerous, and occasionally I was conscious of being followed home to Maryhill Barracks.

I commanded a platoon of people who drove ambulances, staff cars and champs (a kind of Land Rover). We had the highest accident rate in the whole of the United Kingdom. This was because Glasgow's streets were then cobbled because of the trams, and when it rained, these cobbles were very slippery. Most vehicles could cope with this but not the champs. However good the driver, they were unable to stay upright in these conditions. There was nothing we could do.

I had been taught to drive in the army, as officers in the RASC had to hold a driving licence. I well remember not being able to double declutch on the test. The army examiner then demonstrated how it should be done, and said, 'Do it again sir.' I passed. Luckily officers were not allowed to drive even though they had to hold a driving licence. We were always driven by a driver. Nevertheless drivers needed driver training so it was good to be driven around the highlands of Scotland for this purpose.

I enjoyed life in the officers' mess. The food was reasonable and the drinks very cheap. It allowed me to save quite a lot of money for my student days at Oxford. I was able to start running again and encouraged the RASC to enter a team for the Scottish Command Championships in Edinburgh. I organised the team and came second myself in the half-mile.

On Sunday I went to the Episcopalian Cathedral in Glasgow. But one

Sunday to my very great annoyance I was not allowed to go. The captain, who was meant to take three territorial army soldiers on a driving test. passed this duty on to me for dubious reasons. My competence in this area has already been described. Yet I was told to examine people on a driving test, which if passed, would give them a civilian driving licence. It was well known that some people then joined the territorial army as a way of getting such a licence. I decided the only thing to do was to be very strict. I therefore failed two people and passed only one. Nevertheless there could still be one person driving on the roads of Britain today because of my decision.

I sailed through all the church's procedures for selection for ordination. At the end of the 1950s these were very easy for people from my background. I arranged to go to Wells Theological College after Oxford. The Principal of the college did not require any interview. The information that I had been at Shrewsbury School and was going to Oxford University was enough for him to decide.

During the course of my ministry this rightly changed. Indeed a public school education eventually became a disadvantage. I used to tease the Bishop of Southwark's staff team when I was later a member of it. I would introduce myself as the 'token public schoolboy', as for a time I was the only one.

Before going up to Oxford I wrote a letter to the *Shrewsbury Chronicle* urging that Shropshire should take a greater interest in athletics and I began to work with others to form Shrewsbury Athletic Club. A meeting was held and the club was formed. Roger Davies, with whom I had run at school, agreed to run the club with Alderman Tudor Owen as chairman. I captained the Shrewsbury Athletic Club team to victory at their first ever meeting on the Shrewsbury School track. I did what I could to help in the holidays when I returned to Shrewsbury from Oxford. I helped Roger Davies to organise the first two round-the-houses races on New Year's Eve. I competed myself with a team from St Edmund Hall Oxford, where I was captain of cross-country running. It was good to see the club still thriving when I returned to Shrewsbury forty years later.

❧✝❧

CHAPTER 4

An Intelligent Theology

I T was not easy to get used to academic work again after two years in the army. The decision to be ordained resulted in my being more interested in theology than history. It would have been more sensible to have changed the degree course, but that is not easy to do at Oxford. The result was that I was reading as much theology as history, especially in the last two years.

There were two books which helped me considerably at this time. The first was Herbert Butterfield's *Christianity and History*. Part of it dealt with the problem of suffering, which many have found hard to reconcile with a loving God. But Butterfield made it clear 'that only in a world where suffering is possible and vicarious suffering attainable, can human beings measure the heights and depths of love and reach the finer music of life. Because there is tragedy in history love itself is brought to burn with an intenser flame in human experience.' He also warned that 'it is essential not have faith in human nature. Such faith is a recent heresy and a very disastrous one.'[1]

These words were timely as I had just returned from a three week student holiday in Poland where I had visited Auschwitz. It is not difficult to believe in original sin when standing in the gas chamber. Dr Stafford-Clark's[2] definition would often be quoted by me: 'Everyone is born with an innate prejudice in favour of oneself. No one is born with an innate prejudice in favour of other people. The job of religion is to give people that prejudice in favour of other people which they don't naturally have.' Original sin therefore needs to be taken very seriously – not least by religious people.

The other book which helped me was John Knox's *Criticism and Faith*. I had long had difficulty with parts of the Bible. But no one had pointed out the obvious fact that Jesus had to be the final authority rather than the Bible or the Church. John Knox wrote, 'It is not what was written that has authority, but what happened. The Bible has value only because it brings us a first hand account of that happening. The event is the important thing, not the account, and we must interpret the account to recover the event.'³ Biblical Criticism therefore was a way of getting nearer to what actually happened to Jesus. We cannot be fundamentalist about the Bible or the Church – only about the real historical Jesus of Nazareth. This was the insight I needed and would learn more about when I got to Wells.

Meanwhile I was meeting new people, though many from Shrewsbury were also present like Paul Foot and Richard Ingrams. They were soon editing *Parsons Pleasure* which continued the work they had begun on *The Salopian*. The students of St Edmund Hall, however, were known more for their sporting success. There were exceptions of course: John Wells and the future general Sir Michael Rose were also contemporaries of mine.

We were always celebrating the latest sporting success with a splendid dinner in Hall. We won athletics and cross-country running cuppers with a little help from myself. We also won football and rugger and went head of the river in rowing. Canon John Kelly presided over the victory celebrations with great enjoyment and delight. He always gave an exceptionally funny and erudite speech. He was well known as a leading Patristic scholar and for his books on early Christian doctrine and early Christian creeds. He was homosexual and enjoyed the company of young men. He was responsible for reviving the fortunes of the Hall, which though 700 years old, had only just become a college. It had never before had so many undergraduates or such sporting success. John Kelly had made it an Oxford College which was now the equal of others.

I was a member of both the Liddon and Essay Societies. Canon Liddon was a leading Tractarian who had been Vice-Principal of the Hall. He fell out badly with Bishop Gore over the publication of *Lux Mundi*. His influence on the Hall was profound and even in 1958 the three clergy Fellows of the Hall were still in the Tractarian tradition. Evangelicals had not been popular and in 1768 six students were expelled from St Edmund Hall for 'too much religion'. I eventually became president of the Liddon Society and encouraged the discussion of theology, mainly through talks from invited speakers during the year.

The Essay Society met to hear essays written by its own members. I still have the essay which I delivered on 'Pride and Prejudice'. It reveals an important strand of my thinking at the time. The essay starts by commending a remark made by the journalist Walter Lippman that, 'It was our human propensity to insist on having an opinion, when all that we are entitled to have is an open mind.' And yet, I argued, how often do we air our views on world affairs, the bomb, religion, communism, sex and such like questions, as if we really knew enough about those subjects to give a considered opinion? How often does our opinion on these subjects only reflect the 'pride and prejudice' of our particular interests, environment, party, creed or any other system of thought to which we have committed ourselves, rather than a free process of thought entirely independent of these forces?

This was of course partly aimed at the certainty of many Evangelical and Roman Catholic students. It seemed to me then, as it does now, that the certainty embodied in the phrases 'the Bible says' or the 'the Church says' comes from a closed rather than an open mind.

In my second year at Oxford I became joint sacristan with David Gerrard of the chapel at St Edmund Hall. This entitled me to have another year in Hall in a splendid room overlooking the old quad. David and I got to know one another very well. David had come straight from school in Guildford. He was two years younger than me, and was not called up for National Service, which was abolished while I was in the army. It was our destiny to be ordained together, and to work together on many occasions, as will be revealed later in this story. We had a close working relationship with John Cowdrey, the Chaplain, and Graham Midgley, the Dean, who were the Celebrants at Holy Communion each morning. In those days the chapel was well attended mornings, evenings, and especially on Sundays when the Principal was always present.

Each Sunday I also went to High Mass at Pusey House and in my last year was resident there. Hugh Maycock was then the Principal and Donald Allchin was on the staff. I owe both of them a great deal. Hugh would drive me out to Blenheim, which was a terrifying experience, and then we would walk in the park discussing theology. He introduced me to John Robinson's first book *In the End God*. Donald and I would walk to a pub by the river to do the same. I was worried at the time about Hell. How could a good God allow people to be punished eternally? John Robinson's book was a revelation and gave me the answer.

'Christ, in Origen's old words,' says Robinson, 'remains on the Cross as long as one sinner remains in Hell. That is not speculation: it is a statement grounded in the very necessity of God's nature. In a universe of love there can be no heaven which tolerates a chamber of horrors, no hell for any which does not at the same time make it hell for God. He cannot endure that, for *that* would be the final mockery of his nature.'[4]

But Robinson still took seriously the parable of the Sheep and the Goats and the need for choice. However when we *really* see Christ lifted up from the earth drawing us to him on the cross, all is possible. For 'no person in the end can bear that encounter for ever; for it is an encounter with a power than which there can be nothing greater, a meeting with omnipotent Love itself. This love will take no person's choice from him, for it is precisely his choice that it wants. But its will to Lordship is inexhaustible and ultimately unendurable: the sinner *must* yield.'[5]

In 1961 I arrived at Wells Theological College and immediately felt at home. Tom Baker was the Principal and he was quite determined that the students should face and learn from the biblical criticism of the last 150 years. Gradually I became aware that many of the things which had troubled me over the years and from quite a young age, need not have done so.

I had already learnt from John Knox that Jesus Christ was the authority rather than the Church or the Bible. I now realised that biblical criticism was the way to reveal the authentic and authoritative Jesus. The New Testament was written down at different times. The earlier writings being more likely to be accurate than the later ones. The gospels were based on material which was already in existence and was used in worship, the equivalent of the readings we have at services today. These were strung together by the gospel writers at a later date, often to advance their own spin. It was possible therefore to discover what the first preaching (Kerygma) was, and to know which sayings of Jesus were likely to be authentic.

It was very encouraging to find that the first preaching included the Crucifixion and Resurrection which of course was essential for the truth of Christianity. I also found it helpful that some of the things which I found difficult to believe were written down later. These were therefore either considered by the writers to be secondary, or were possibily not authentic at all. What mattered was that the essential things were preached in the earliest days.

I was also introduced to Rudolf Bultmann, Paul Tillich and Joseph Fletcher. My excitement in reading these theologians was not because I agreed with all they said, but because they were tackling the problems I had long wrestled with, and were not afraid to follow the truth wherever it led them.

Bultmann[6] was so distressed by what many army chaplains told him, about the almost total lack of impact their preaching made upon young soldiers in their charge in the second world war, that he determined to alert the Church to what he believed was the root of the trouble. This was that the Christian Gospel needed radical reinterpretation before it could become a faith to live by in the twentieth century. This enterprise he called 'demythologising', which, in spite of its negative side, is in fact a very positive and constructive undertaking.

Bultmann of course does not use the word myth in the popular sense of a fairy story. Myth means a story which may or may not be historically true, but whose chief purpose is to explain a truth that lies beyond it. Bultmann would say the New Testament interprets the meaning of Jesus Christ in mythological language of this kind. But today we no longer find the mythology helpful. So, says Bultmann, the myth has to be taken out of Christianity so that the truth which lies behind the gospel stories may shine forth.

What we have to do therefore with the mythological statements of the New Testament is to try to discover the basic experience which underlies them. If we can truly share and make them our own, then we can share the faith of the New Testament even though we reject the thought forms in which it is set.

Let us try and see very briefly how this works. The Christian gospel declares people are fallen and in the grip of evil powers. Satan and his host cause us to sin and are responsible for our alienation from God. We are helpless in the grip of evil agencies. This has little meaning for us today. But if we 'demythologise' and get at the basic experience behind the thought forms of the first century, we get something like this: We are in the grip of our own desire to achieve security and control our future in our own way; we look to visible and tangible things to give security like money, pleasure, power and ambition. But because all these things are transitory, and life is essentially insecure, people who base their lives on these things are always prisoners. Moreover we are bound to achieve our security and answer our own future at the expense of other people's efforts to do the same. Hence arise anger, jealousy and all kinds of strife and bitterness. Such persons have lost their freedom and are slaves to their own anxieties, cannot be themselves and then cannot give themselves to others in love. All this is what the New Testament calls Sin and being possessed by Devils.

The opposite of this in New Testament language is Redemption or being in the Spirit; that is to say being released from the tyranny of the Evil power, Sin and Death and being filled with one supernatural kind of strength coming down from above. Demythologised, this means being open to the future, being released from the past and its guilt, no longer being compelled to carve a niche for ourselves to secure our future, but being prepared to abandon it trustingly into the hand of God.

It is also freedom from the compulsion to win recognition by our own efforts instead of being allowed to receive it as a gift, to be bold enough to allow God to accept us as we are, because He loves us, not because of anything we have to show which might appear to earn his acceptance. Thus we are free from anxiety, and so are able to enter into fellowship with others on the basis of generous, self-giving love. This is the life of Faith – the life of the Spirit.

However we cannot change from one state to the other by our own efforts, but only by encountering a compelling and liberating word or assurance which comes from outside ourselves. For Bultmann firmly believed it was only through the Cross and Resurrection of Jesus that we finally get the power to change from one state to the other. True, Bultmann did not see the need to stress the historicity of the two events, and for this he has been much criticised. Nevertheless he never denied the Resurrection – indeed no Christian could, in my view, and remain a real Christian. He has been very sceptical about the resurrection appearances and the bodily resurrection of Christ. But he believes what is essential, that Christ was alive after his death and did indeed conquer death. The important thing for Bultmann was not whether it could be proved historically, but whether people found it to be true here and now in their own experience. For this is how we come to know the truth of the Resurrection.

Tillich[7] was also influenced by the first world war when he was himself an army chaplain. In experiencing life, says Tillich we experience concern. We are concerned about our work, daily bread, personal relationships and many other things. In our concern we experience anxiety. For all our concerns are finite and transitory. We ourselves face finitude and transitoriness. We may try to dodge this with a cynical unconcern, a dogmatic and easy self-assurance, but we know in our hearts we are not being honest. In the end we shall not dodge death.

This anxiety, this fear of death, is manifested as a particular sickness in our society. We have a deep insecurity, coupled with hostility towards others, towards ourselves, towards God. We are afraid of life, oppressed with its meaninglessness. Tillich says that this insecurity and hostility indicate what he called Estrangement. Tillich unlike St Paul never used the word Sin. An Estrangement from others, from self and from God also indicates unacceptability. We are unable to accept ourselves or to feel ourselves accepted.

This is the universal predicament of human beings. It is the same predicament at which so much twentieth century art is pointing. Joyce, Eliot, Auden, Sartre, Camus, Arthur Miller, Tennessee Williams point to it. Many modern plays and novels express the meaninglessness, the deep-seated anxiety that humans feel because of this Estrangement, the lack of the ability to communicate deep things to each other, the guilt, the despair that lies beneath the surface of so much modern life.

All this of course the Gospels said long ago. The trouble is that the New Testament is so buried in the thought forms and language of a different age that modern people cannot see it. For Tillich therefore, Jesus is the New Being. The person who brings in a new state of affairs and brings us alive. The miracles that Jesus performed were symbols of the New Power that is in the world. The Cross and Resurrection though historical, are again mainly symbols of the New Being. The Cross proclaims that Jesus through his suffering and death participated to the full in our Estrangement. Yet Jesus, unlike us, was not Estranged – He conquered. The separation He experienced never overcame the unity between Himself and God, between Himself and humankind, between Him and Himself.

The Resurrection proclaims that the power of the New Being – the power of the selfless love of the Cross is victorious. God is God. He is stronger than anxiety, meaninglessness, suffering, despair and death. What we need is to be grasped ourselves by the New Being in Christ, for this is what atonement is. For when we are grasped by the New Being we are healed, reconciled to God, to one another and to ourselves. Guilt is taken away. We are accepted, and we are enabled to accept ourselves. We lose anxiety and find the courage to live.

This is an experience which countless millions of Christians have had. It is an experience which can be ours if we have faith. It is an experience which was also mine. This of course does not mean believing in something which cannot be proved. It has never meant that in genuine religion. Faith means surrendering ourselves freely and trustingly, in spite of our great doubts and with open eyes into the hands of God so that he can make us whole. For it is only when we have completely surrendered ourselves to Him, when we have confessed our faults to Him, only then can we be grasped by the power of His healing grace, by the power of the New Being, and have peace of mind.

Such a faith, says Tillich, is more like courage. The courage first of all to throw ourselves into the hands of God, in spite of all the objections that can be raised against such a course. The courage also, once this is done, to accept the fact that we are accepted by God and to continue to live our lives in this conviction. So that at length the knowledge of our acceptance penetrates the innermost depths of our being and we can at last give ourselves completely to God and others.

Finally Joseph Fletcher's[8] important contribution to the new morality was known about at Wells long before he wrote *Situation Ethics* in 1966. 'Love', for Fletcher, is the only 'norm' to be used in deciding a course of action. This is of course 'Love' as defined in the New Testament, for it is only as we steep ourselves in Jesus's Love, that we can then apply it to the situations we encounter.

The method of *Situation Ethics* can be found in what St Paul said to the saints at Philippi:

And this I pray, that your Love may abound yet more and more in knowledge and in all judgement.

Here in a few words, says Fletcher, are the four pillars of the method of Christian Ethics, in the order of the Apostle's words:

1. A prayerful reliance upon God's grace.
2. The law of Love as norm.
3. Knowledge of the facts, of the empirical situation in all its variety and relativity and particularity.
4. Judgement, i.e. decision – which is a matter of responsibility in humility.

This is not Antinomianism. General rules are still helpful so long as 'Love' as defined in the New Testament has the final say. For sometimes such 'Love' does say, break the rules.

A good example of this was Dietrich Bonhoeffer who was involved in the plot to kill Hitler. Bonhoeffer was a distinguished theologian who was also a modern Christian Ethicist. He was executed for his part in the plot. In Tegel prison yard he was questioned by a fellow-prisoner and asked how he justified what he had done. Bonhoeffer replied, 'If he, as a pastor, saw a drunken driver racing at high speed down the kurfursten-damm, he did not consider it his only or his main duty to bury the victims of the madman, or to comfort the relatives; it was important to wrench the wheel out of the hands of the drunkard.' What Bonhoeffer did was what Jesus's 'Love' told him to do in the situation he was in.[9]

Time passed very pleasantly at Wells. We lived in the oldest complete street in England in small medieval houses where we also dined. In winter we played hockey as there were not enough of us to field both a football and rugby team. However some of us did occasionally play for the local rugby club. In summer tennis was played on secluded courts near the cathedral and I captained the college team.

We worshipped in a chapel in the cathedral and I especially enjoyed the half hour period of meditation each morning sitting at the back of the cathedral. This followed Mattins and the Eucharist. We would go for a drink most days after Evensong or before Compline. Many of us got to know Peggy the barmaid at the Crown Inn. She knew and encouraged succeeding generations of students and on a famous occasion swam the moat outside the Bishop's Palace with two students.

At Wells I became a Christian Socialist. I was influenced by Mervyn Stockwood, Trevor Huddleston and Dietrich Bonhoeffer. As we have seen, Bonhoeffer opposed Hitler from the early 1930s, but the majority of Christians kept out of politics and so failed to prevent the evil of the gas chambers. It was important we all learned the right lesson from this, and were fully engaged in politics. Only in this way could we influence the political debate and prevent racism from getting a real grip in England as it had in Germany. We also needed to bring the good news of the Gospel to the poor, marginalized and excluded, as the Bible demanded. For I came to see that the God of the Scriptures always sees the affliction of people, whether they are in Egypt at the time of Moses, or in Britain's inner cities and the world today. But God depends on us responding, as Moses did, in liberating the poor and oppressed, and as Martin Luther King and Archbishop Desmond Tutu have in our own day.

But we need also to copy the determination of the Biblical people of Israel to build a just and fair society in the Promised Land. The attempt was made to exclude poverty by law: every seven years debts were cancelled, and every fifty years the family home, if lost, could be recovered. Strangers, unlike in England today, were cared for and made welcome.

In the end this attempt failed. Again, like the United Kingdom of today, the rich began to get richer and the poor poorer. The Old Testament prophets warned that this was wrong and was sowing the seeds for the destruction of Jerusalem. Nevertheless the prophets in the Bible still spoke of a Messiah who would one day bring good news to the poor and establish justice and righteousness (Isaiah 61.1).

Jesus at the beginning of his ministry identifies himself with this same passage and the whole jubilee tradition which I have just outlined. He reads the passage from Isaiah in the synagogue at Nazareth (Luke 4) which identifies him as God's chosen one who will bring good news to the poor. 'Today' says Jesus, 'this passage of scripture has come true.' Nothing could therefore be more central to what Jesus is about.

The Bible then shows us how Jesus demonstrated this through his actions. Throughout his ministry he chose to be a friend of all those who were last in the society of his day. He spent most of his time with the poor, the marginalized, the excluded, lepers, outcasts, tax gatherers and sinners. Jesus ate with these people and stayed in their houses. He healed them, told parables about them and said one day they would be first and not last.

We learn therefore from the Bible that to follow Jesus must mean standing by the poor, the marginalized and the excluded. From my time at Wells onwards I found this particularly important in a society where most people have become rich, comfortable and powerful, because they form a majority of the Electorate, and vote at General Elections mostly in their own interests. The leaders of the political parties know this, and believe there are no votes in helping the poor and marginalized. This is a cancer at the heart of our society. A dictatorship by a rich and powerful majority which excludes the poor minority from having any real voice is a very horrid thing, even when it happens in a democracy and through the ballot box. This is why the gap between rich and poor grows ever wider. At Wells I hoped the Labour Party under Harold Wilson would change this, but I now believe that the comfortable majority will ensure no political party makes the changes that would prove really effective.

It always seems extraordinary to me that Evangelicals in the early 1960s could not see what the Bible was clearly saying. Later as we shall see, some Evangelicals read their Bibles more attentively. But in the 1960s they were very dismissive of what they saw as the Social Gospel, as some remain dismissive today.

Towards the end of my time at Wells, Bishop John Robinson's book *Honest to God* was published in March 1963. I was overjoyed. At last the cat was out of the bag. This was the significance of the book. From then on clergy and most importantly lay people would have some idea of what was going on in the world of academic theology. Bultmann, Tillich, Bonhoeffer and Fletcher would be known about and read. And the interest was phenomenal. 'No new book of serious theology has sold so quickly in the history of the world,' claimed David Edwards the editor and managing director of the publishers SCM Press.[10]

The Evangelicals were of course furious. But their criticism only had the effect of giving further publicity to the book. At last an open and honest debate was taking place in the national press, and the debate would go on in the Church for most of the Sixties. In the words of one national newspaper, 'It is an agonising and unusual spectacle, a Bishop groping for truth, admitting that he does not know all the answers.'

At the same time I was visiting Tony Tremlett, Vicar of St Stephen Rochester Row Westminster. Tom Baker had suggested him as my training incumbent. We met and disagreed about almost everything. He was a Conservative in politics and theology but in spite of this we got on well. We talked, drank whisky and disagreed late into the night, but we enjoyed it. Next day at breakfast with the six curates, I made it clear that, if I came, so did Bultmann, Bonhoeffer and Tillich. I think they hoped I would not come, but Tony Tremlett did invite me, and I accepted. It proved to be the right decision. For at no time did Tony ever try to change my views, but he did enable me to put the new theology across in a better and therefore more effective way.

CHAPTER 5

※ ✝ ※

Westminster and Marriage

I WAS ordained deacon and priest in St Paul's Cathedral on Trinity Sundays in 1963 and 1964. I was the seventh curate on a staff team of ten at St Stephen Rochester Row, Westminster. For as well as the seven curates and Vicar, there were two nuns from the Deaconess Community of St Andrew. We all wore cassocks everywhere, especially in the street, to show we were Anglicans! Westminster's Roman Catholic Cathedral was in the parish, and as Roman Catholic priests are forbidden by law to wear cassocks in the street, it followed that anyone wearing a cassock was an Anglican. This, anyway, was how the Vicar Tony Tremlett saw it.

Life was very full. I opened the gates of the church at 6.30 a.m. every morning. Mattins, the Eucharist and Meditation followed. We were required to do at least 30 visits a week which we noted down and reported on at the weekly staff meeting. I was also Chaplain to a large boys club, called St Andrews Home & Club, where I was expected to spend some time. I managed a football team and persuaded the guitar group to play at the annual service at St Stephens. This was very new in 1964 and the church was packed. Andrew Lloyd Webber was interested and came to give help and support. He was a boy at Westminster School at the time, but it would not be long before he composed *Jesus Christ Superstar*.

The debate about *Honest to God* was still raging and I found there was a great deal of interest in the book from people who did not attend church. So with the help of Rene Dicker I formed a discussion group of non-Christians who wished to study the book, and in particular the theologians whom John Robinson had brought to their attention. Rene Dicker was a member of the congregation who had studied theology at university and was now a teacher. We were assisted by Professor Christopher Evans, an eminent New Testament theologian at King's College London who lived in the parish. He also became my spiritual director and his advice and help was invaluable. The playwright Tom Stoppard came to one of the meetings of the *Honest to God* group. This resulted in my getting to know him and being asked to baptise his first child. The group continued for three years during which two people became Christians, and others grew very sympathetic.

A whole morning would be spent each week taking the Reserved Sacrament to people who were sick or housebound. One of the nuns would walk in front of me as I held the Sacrament. She would go inside the home to prepare everything whilst I waited outside. I would then enter, take a short service and administer the Sacrament. I then left, leaving the nun to clear up before following her to the next house. The whole procedure now seems extraordinary, especially as I was not allowed to have any conversation with the person receiving the Sacrament.

We were all doing what had been laid down by the previous Vicar George Reindorp. He had written a book called *The Parish comes Alive* which was very influential. Tony Tremlett therefore kept things as they were, and as a consequence we all worked much too hard. George Reindorp used to boast that all his curates got ulcers. It was not as bad under Tremlett. Nevertheless no curate would put up with it today.

In the evening there were a number of parish clubs and activities to attend or organise. After that we would often go for a drink in Bermondsey. Tony did not mind us drinking but we were not allowed to go to pubs in the parish. The people of Bermondsey therefore saw quite a lot of us, especially the pubs with good music groups. I remember on one occasion the music group striking up 'All Things Bright and Beautiful', as six of us curates walked into the pub wearing cassocks. Bermondsey people were very generous to priests in the 1960s. I hardly ever paid for a drink. People we did not know would offer to pay simply because we were wearing a cassock.

I joined the Westminster Labour Party and began to attend ward party meetings though I would never go canvassing in the parish. Most of Millbank was then council houses and voted Labour, whilst Ashley Gardens, Vincent and Smith Square were Conservative. I often visited the Roman Catholic Cathedral and got to know the Administrator Monsignor Bartlett very well. He taught me the difference between Irish and English Catholicism. English Catholicism was much closer to Anglicanism because it had its roots in the English aristocracy which had kept catholicism alive over the centuries. He was very keen that the English variety flourished at Westminster. I particularly enjoyed lunching in the cathedral clergy house where nuns cooked delicious food even in Lent.

I got on well with the Roman Catholic clergy, partly because this was

the time of the second Vatican Council and ecumenical relations were at
their most enthusiastic following the impact made by Pope John XXIII.
The Westminster Christian Council had recently been formed with
representatives from all the denominations. I was a member alongside
representatives from Westminster Abbey, Westminster Cathedral, the
Methodist Central Hall, St Martin's in the Fields, St James Picadilly, the
Baptist Church and all the major churches in Westminster except for
Martin Lloyd-Jones and the hardline Evangelicals at Westminster
Chapel. The latter was famous for his one hour minimum length
sermons!

The Week of Prayer for Christian Unity in those days witnessed huge
processions of people marching from Trafalgar Square to St Paul's
Cathedral. The only opposition, apart from Martin Lloyd-Jones, came
from the Reverend Ian Paisley. He brought people from Northern
Ireland to protest at what he saw as a very worrying development. I
remember remonstrating with him in Trafalgar Square and telling him
to get back to the sixteenth century.

At that time he could be written off as having no influence on
mainstream Christianity. None of us could have guessed that the future
lay with Paisley's kind of Evangelical Fundamentalism. It is appalling to
see the position of power he has now, and, compared with our own
Conservative Evangelicals, he no longer seems extreme. The enthusiasm
for Christian Unity would fade almost to nothing, but more and more
people would be attracted to the simplistic Gospel of the Evangelicals.

In 1967 John Stott organised the National Evangelical Congress at
Keele which over a thousand people attended. John Stott declared in a
preparatory speech,[1] 'We have acquired a reputation for narrow
partisanship and obstructionism. We have to acknowledge this, and for
the most part we have no one but ourselves to blame.' Keele marked a
turning point for Evangelicals, particularly those in the Church of
England. From now on they were determined to gain positions of power
within the Church rather than outside it. At first this was to mean
moderate Evangelicals, but as we shall see, in the end Keele opened the
floodgates for Evangelical Fundamentalists as well.

In 1965 Tony Tremlett left St Stephen's to become Bishop of Dover. He
had enjoyed life in Westminster not least because he was surrounded by
seven young curates. Tony was gay but completely celibate as most
homosexual priests were in those days. Because of this perhaps he would
sometimes get depressed. There was a time when he did not speak to his
curates for two weeks! Nevertheless as chaplain of Trinity Hall

Cambridge and at St Stephen's he was responsible for an amazing number of people being ordained. He rightly used his homosexuality as a gift which God had given him and which enabled him to communicate well with young men. As Bishop of Dover he was less happy, as he did not even have a chaplain, let alone seven curates.

Bill Davidson was the next Vicar but he was unpopular with some of the congregation. I was now the senior curate, and I did my best to support him when he was criticised. It was wrong, however, to do so over the church spire which was about to fall down. It could either be partially demolished and capped, or re-built. I argued that the money it would take to rebuild the spire could be better spent. This was an error of judgment. Nevertheless for many years the spire was capped and looked very unsightly. At the time it seemed a waste of money to do anything else, but we had forgotten what important symbols spires are for all people, not least those who do not attend church. Eventually another vicar rebuilt the spire which I was then glad to see.

A person who gave me very good advice was Bishop Montgomery-Campbell who lived in Vincent Square in retirement. He was looked after by his daughter Jane, whom I was to meet again in Shrewsbury when I retired. He had previously been Bishop of London. He came to evening prayer at 6 p.m. every weekday evening, and sometimes I would walk with him back to his house for a sherry and a chat. This would take quite a long time as he needed to clear the pavement of leaves with his walking stick as he went along. However he still had a very lively mind and I enjoyed hearing his stories for which he was famous. My favourite story concerned Mervyn Stockwood, the Bishop of Southwark who was known for being a rather flamboyant Prince Bishop. Bishop Henry came across him wearing his full canonicals at a Buckingham Palace garden party and said, 'Ah Mervyn, incognito I see!'

It was at this time I met my future wife Ann Coburn. Many young women came to St Stephens, most of whom were either nurses or Foreign Office girls. Westminster Hospital was in the parish and every curate visited a ward each week. We also attended Matron's Ball which was a very grand affair. All seven curates, dressed in black cassocks, descended a majestic staircase and were greeted by matron at the bottom. Then of course we chose a suitable girl and started dancing. We always made quite a dash in the eightsome reel when all of us took part.

Ann Coburn however worked as a secretary at the Foreign Office. We met first at a parish party given by one of the Churchwardens and his wife, Lieutenant Colonel Jim and Dorothy Haywood. I spotted Ann's face on the other side of the room and it really was love at first sight. It was the Sixties and she wore a mini skirt which really showed off her legs to perfection. She lived with two other Foreign Office girls in a flat in Pimlico.

We started going out and within six months I proposed. But she was not certain. She wanted to go to the embassy in Brazil. She had not been at the Foreign Office long and wanted to travel. Once she married, the rule then was she had to resign. In the end she did not go to Brazil but to the embassy in Paris. She only stayed six months and when she returned I proposed again and she accepted.

The hesitation was not surprising, for in marrying a priest, especially 40 years ago, one risked taking on more than marriage. I tried to explain to Ann what was involved, especially for someone who was not as committed a Christian as I was.

In fact Ann always met the expectations of parishioners in each of the parishes where I was Vicar. Not that parishioners have the right to any expectation of a vicar's wife. Today congregations mostly understand this, but it was not so then. Ann went to church throughout my active ministry. People enjoyed talking to her and were helped by her. She assisted with the Sunday School, the refreshments and ran a woman's club. She was the Virgin Mary in the Christmas Nativity play with our baby son Peter as Jesus, and did all the things clergy wives do. So hesitation was in order.

We were married in Glossop Parish Church in Derbyshire where Ann was brought up. Her father and mother were both doctors. James Coburn was a Consultant Dermatologist in Manchester. He was born in Glasgow and met Ann's mother Sheila Bowden when they were both medical students at Manchester University. The Bowdens had lived in Glossop since the sixteenth century. We still have the will of Samuel Bowden, a farmer who was born in 1703. Sheila's father and grandfather were both Registrars for Glossop and keen Methodists. Sheila's mother Clara Greenwood was an Anglican and taught in the local Church of England school.

Ann's father and mother did not go to church. James died when he was only 53 on holiday in Paris. Sheila was a strong woman and a magistrate in Glossop for many years. She was one of the first doctors to be involved in family planning and was a strong advocate of abortion. Anyone who questioned the right of a woman to have an abortion in all circumstances was immediately made aware of their very grave error. Ann was the eldest in the family. Her brother Peter was two years younger and also became a Consultant Dermatologist. Her sister Alison was fifteen years younger and later became one of the leaders of the charity 'Common Purpose'.

Ann went to two Church of England schools, the Duke of Norfolk's school in Glossop, later boarding at St Elphin's school in Darley Dale. Unlike her parents Ann did go to church. It may not have been very willingly, as a teacher at her school used to call at Ann's house to take her. At St Elphin's attending church was of course compulsory. However Ann continued to go when she came to London. This is just as well as otherwise I might never have met her.

Ann has often been critical of the institutional church and doubtful about Christianity. She found the views of Conservative Christians on gay people and women the last straw. She had little patience with the Church of England, as it failed to stand up to the religious bullies, especially on equal opportunities for gay people in the church.

When we met she was reading *The True Wilderness* by Harry Williams. She found the book helpful, as did John Osborne, who recommended it as one of his books of the year. Harry Williams wrote as a person who had faced his demons. He was Dean of Trinity Hall Cambridge and later a Mirfield Monk. He discovered through a process of analysis that he was worshipping a monster of a God. He realised that behind the façade of much worship and good works he unconsciously harboured the demon of guilt feelings. In spite of his intellectual and theological sophistication he was caught in the demon's claws. He was not the only Christian who needed to be freed to be fully human and so be embraced by the real love of Christ. This resulted in Harry being one of the first Christians to openly live as a gay man. He wrote about this in his autobiography *Some Day I'll Find You*, and he had a profound influence on many.

The experience I remember most as a Curate was visiting a ward at the Westminster Children's Hospital. There was a girl of twelve dying of cancer called Vanessa, whom we Curates used to visit. She knew she was dying, and was often in pain, and yet she was one of the happiest people I have ever known. The philosopher Bertrand Russell said this was a situation which should destroy one's faith in God. But it did the opposite. Certainly we all went to see her feeling angry with God for what was happening. But we came away uplifted by Vanessa's own strong faith. The nurses and doctors were similarly moved and affected. She was confirmed in hospital, and received Holy Communion regularly till she died. Her parents, who were not believers, became Christians because of the faith Vanessa had shown.

This was not an isolated experience. Clergy are privileged to see people at their most vulnerable moments, and to witness what Christ can do for those who truly believe. Sometimes the healing miracle, much trumpeted by some Evangelicals, does occur. When this happens, there are usually psychosomatic reasons, but I have not found such incidents as miraculous as the experience of people, like Vanessa, who are given strength to face real suffering and triumph over it.

❧✝❧

CHAPTER 6

A South Bank Priest

I N 1968 I went to see Bishop John Robinson because I wanted to be a priest in the Diocese of Southwark. I was attracted by South Bank religion for which Southwark was famous, and had always admired the Bishop of Southwark as well as John.

The South Bank had long been associated with radicalism. The Reverend John Ball preached a famous sermon on Blackheath Common at the start of the Peasants Revolt in 1381.[1] 'Why do they use us thus?' He cried 'Why do they hold us in bondage? Are we not descended from the same parents Adam and Eve?'

It was also a place of freedom for good or ill. Hence the bear baiting, the Rose and Globe theatres, the plays of Shakespeare and Marlowe. The Bishop of Winchester licensed prostitutes near his Palace which was close to Southwark Cathedral. They were called Winchester geese. William Blake had his famous vision in Peckham, and lived near the automated dark satanic Albion Mill in the Blackfriars Road. It was deliberately burned down by South Londoners afraid for their jobs. Christian leaders of the Chartist Movement helped to lead a mass revolt on Kennington Common. The Clapham sect, William Wilberforce, and Octavia Hill brought good news to the slaves of the empire and the poor of South London long before the leaders of South Bank religion.

I was encouraged by the radicalisation of South London and wanted to be part of the innovation that was taking place in theology, ethics, and parish life. Eric James agreed to show me the parish of St Michael and All Angels and All Souls with Emmanuel Camberwell. Eric had also been a curate at St Stephen's Rochester Row. He was then a canon of Southwark Cathedral with oversight of the riverside parishes.

As indicated by its lengthy title the parish was the result of a recent amalgamation of three parishes. This amalgamation resulted in twenty parishioners worshipping in a decaying Victorian building which could hold 600 people. The situation was so desperate that the remaining parishioners were prepared for any experiment, any challenge.

In May 1968 I was therefore instituted as Parish Priest of St Michael and All Angels and All Souls with Emmanuel Camberwell by Bishop John Robinson. The Parish Council rapidly took two major decisions: the first was to establish links with the neighbouring church of St Paul Newington. The second was to move from their church and build another more suitable to their needs. Upon the realisation of these two decisions hung the ability of the church to play a major role in revitalising the religious and community development of the area.

The parochial system has many strengths, including being rooted in the realities of the local situation. It has corresponding weaknesses, especially in the inner city. St Michael's and St Paul's were both sited in a decaying area which was being comprehensively redeveloped into a huge new housing estate, the Brandon estate. The parochial boundary split the estate. The parish showed no corresponding identity with the rebuilt communities. Separate parishes breed isolation among the clergy and congregations. They create fear and suspicion of outsiders. They prevent shared use of valuable resources. Consequently there has been a search for new structures which maintain the strength of the parochial system while overcoming its weaknesses.

In March 1969 David Gerrard was inducted as Vicar of St Paul's Newington. I had mentioned to Bishop John Robinson that David wished to come to Southwark and I was sure we could work well together. So David was invited to come to St Paul's with that in view. He brought with him his wit and humour which became legendary in the Diocese, especially when he spoke at Diocesan Synod. Before he left Hampstead where he was a curate, he was filmed for television walking in leafy Hampstead accusing the local residents of 'intellectual incest'.

Both parishes now began to debate the best form of parochial reorganisation, and by the autumn it was clear the overwhelming number of parishioners were in favour of Group ministry. It was to be two years before the legal formalities were completed, but effectively the Group ministry began in September 1969.

Group ministry meant that the two parishes bound themselves together in a federation. The clergy met for a staff meeting every week. A Group Council was formed, with two lay people elected by each Parochial Church Council, and four other Christians who worked in the area who could contribute their help and advice. They included a church school Head Teacher, a Methodist Minister, a Roman Catholic Educational Welfare Officer and an Educational Psychologist.

The establishment of the Group ministry resulted in an immediate boost to both churches. Morale was raised by undertaking new projects like the local community newspaper *Compass* which sold 2,000 copies each month in the local area, or taking 150 people away for the weekend to plan for the future. New members, most of them young, were attracted into the church. The number of church members grew every year as did their spirit and enthusiasm. The congregation at St Michael eventually grew to over 100 adults and fifty young people and children.

This was partly due to the decision of the St Michael's Parochial Church Council to leave their large Victorian church. The decision to move was forced upon them by the unwieldy size of the building and the enormous costs needed to restore and maintain it. The church was also poorly sited in the parish. It was isolated from the new estates and therefore it was decided to rebuild the church on a new site.

St Michael's church secondary school was situated centrally in the parish. It was planned to expand it into a large church comprehensive school by amalgamating it with another secondary school. After considerable discussion with the school governors, the Diocesan Board of Education, the Inner London Education Authority and the Department of Education and Science, the Parochial Church Council agreed to build the new church on the expanded site of the new school. The name of the school was to be the Archbishop Michael Ramsey School after the then Archbishop of Canterbury, who took a great interest in the project. The parish paid the total cost of the new church from the sale of the old one. The new school was also a centre of the community. Teachers stayed behind after school to run club and youth activities for the whole neighbourhood. The buildings were used most evenings not only by the church and school but also by the St John Ambulance, tenants associations and other organisations.

The first decision made by the Group Council was that the care of individual Christians and the church family by the clergy should never be neglected in favour of social or political activism. It is a prevalent temptation for radical priests to concentrate on social case work and community development while neglecting the worship and teaching of their own congregations. This results in declining, ignorant and apathetic congregations who are unwilling and unable to contribute anything towards helping their local community and solving its problems. The Church must involve itself in all the difficulties, disadvantages and problems found in inner city areas. But these problems will only be affected by lively Christian congregations acting out their Christian beliefs in the situation in which they live.

The central action of the Christian family is to meet together around the Lord's table, and to worship together in the Eucharist. Through a Joint Liturgical Committee, the involvement of the laity in readings, intercessions and thanksgiving, through modern musical settings and joint worship on special occasions, the centrality of worship has permeated both churches. Joint retreats, pilgrimages and weekends away for study and learning were well attended, and greatly strengthened the congregation on its return to Camberwell. This enabled them to realise they existed not only to bring people to a belief in God and to worship Him, but also to send people out of the churches to become involved in local affairs as part of their involvement in the kingdom of God.

David Gerrard and I wrote about what was achieved in a book called *Urban Ghetto* which was published by Lutterworth Press in 1976. I will not repeat here what we wrote, except to say that we were convinced of both what the local church could do on its own in the inner city, and what the national church could do to assist. The book really called for a *Faith in the City* report, ten years before it eventually happened.

We wrote then that in order to eliminate poverty in our urban ghettos we need a crusade for human hope and dignity for those who have been denied them. Unless people from all areas, professions and interests combine together in a new vision of the future, there are no prospects of any radical changes to our society.

The Church which has such a vision must form one group campaigning for change. It has the advantage of workers both in the urban ghettos and throughout the nation. It works with all people of all classes. It should comfort the afflicted and afflict the comfortable. Historically, religion has been a conservative influence, a stabilising force. It has provided society with a comprehensive scheme of meaning, a universal framework within which particular social institutions, convictions, values and practices find their significance, and which gives them their ultimate justification. Religion overarches society as a sacred canopy.

The Church must withdraw its sanctification of our society with its destructive differentiation between the overfed and the undernourished, the rich and the poor. Our society provides little individual fulfilment and few balanced communities. The church must work to build a better society based on creative intelligence, designed to increase the quality of living for all its members. The Church must work to influence the political and moral attitudes and behaviour of its members to redress intolerable wrongs. The Church must shape and share its vision of the future with teachers and journalists, politicians and planners, community leaders and unionists, with all groups and individuals who care about justice.

It must do this as a national institution working with other national bodies, and more importantly, on a local parochial level. The Church is one of the few bodies working in the inner city which has not been overcome by disillusionment and despair at the enormity of the problem. This is not only due to its own inherently optimistic vision and faith, but also because it is by its very nature rooted in the locality.

Radical change can only occur in the inner city if it is precipitated by a united effort from inside and outside the ghetto. The inner city must be treated as a priority area. The inner city environment will never be transformed by mere government initiatives, nor by the sole efforts of its inhabitants, however heroic they may be. It is a problem so vast, with so many causes, such a complex web of deprivation, such a history of failure, that it can never be solved by politicians, social workers, teachers or clergy, all acting on their own. The problem can only be solved by united action, and only if the conscience of the nation is aroused to the desperate plight and gross deprivation of millions of its most power-less members. This is a good description of the *Faith in the City* report which was published in 1985. A report I was eventually to have a part in implementing.

Meanwhile I got to know well a Methodist minister who had lived in inner city Camberwell since the early 1920s. Jimmy Butterworth was a legend who had appeared on the television programme 'This is Your Life'. He turned his Methodist Church into a hugely successful youth club which he called Clubland. It was the first mixed youth club in the country and he ran it on public school lines. The monitors wore gowns when they processed into chapel in front of Jimmy. This still happened in the early 1970s when I went there to preach. Jimmy was well over the usual retirement age when I met him and no longer the force he once was, but he could not give it up. He enjoyed a glass of sherry with me in his study while he told me of his amazing exploits.

He still attended every Arsenal football match home and away with the chairman. He told me about his conversations with George Best and other leading players who all knew him. The whole Arsenal football team would visit Clubland in Camberwell which was a great encouragement to local young people. An amazing number of old boys and girls would come back for the service on Sunday evening. He would often preach on the importance of 'Christianity' rather than 'Churchianity'. He was a member of the Group Council but by then he had little to contribute.

Though I enjoyed and liked Jimmy, he was the classic example of someone who should have retired at the proper time. As it was, he gradually saw all that he had built up fall apart and crumble. His successor had little choice but to turn it back into a Methodist Church again.

Ted Maidment, a future headmaster of Shrewsbury School, can remember every detail of his stay at Clubland. Ted, as a teacher at Lancing College, accompanied boys to Camberwell because St Michael's parish is also the Lancing College Mission. Ted has a photographic memory and was one of my allies at Lancing, along with Robin Reeve, a future headmaster of King's School Wimbledon. Both assisted me in introducing Lancing boys, and eventually girls, to the realities of inner city life.

Trevor Huddleston, when he was at Lancing, was first introduced to social deprivation on visits to St Michael's parish during the depression in 1931. I knew, from my own experience of Shrewsbury House in Liverpool, the importance of such links, not so much to the people of Camberwell, but to the public schoolboys of Lancing. I therefore organised four-day Social Studies courses in Camberwell for Lancing College pupils. Many attended and were greatly influenced, not least Jonathan Lloyd, who later became Director of Social Responsibility in the Southwark Diocese. In return Robin Reeve, Ted Maidment and boys from Lancing, organised a summer holiday club for local children in Camberwell.

Lancing's link with the parish led to a strong link with the new Archbishop Michael Ramsey Comprehensive School, whose pupils opted to attend the Social Studies course together with pupils from Lancing. A teacher from the college became a Governor, and eventually Archbishop Michael Ramsey School joined Lancing as a member of the Woodard Corporation, the first Church of England comprehensive school to do so.

David Sheppard succeeded John Robinson as Bishop of Woolwich in 1970. David had captained England at cricket and was a moderate Evangelical. Mervyn Stockwood was surprisingly one of the first bishops to appoint Evangelicals to senior positions in the church. This was a significant moment, for although most of the early appointments were of moderate men, it led in the end to the appointment of Conservative Evangelical bishops who would start to change the nature of the Church of England.

However David Sheppard believed in the Social Gospel, and was also influential in persuading other Evangelicals to do the same. David

himself was influenced by a remarkable layman at Brandon Baptist
Church who lived not far from my vicarage. His name was Roger
Dowley, and he wrote a very important book called *Towards the recovery
of a lost bequest – a layman's work – notes on the biblical pattern for a just
community*. The main thrust of the notes was to prove to Evangelicals in
particular that they had neglected the Lost Bequest of the Social Gospel,
which the Bible made very clear, if only they read it properly. He, David
Sheppard, and others at this time made it difficult for future Evangelicals
to ignore the Social Gospel.

The change from John Robinson to David Sheppard was still
considerable. The dynamism and thrust of Mervyn Stockwood's first ten
years in Southwark was as much due to his choice of John Robinson as
Bishop of Woolwich as to his own radicalism. And John clothed that
radicalism in a theology. John and Mervyn had worked together in
Bristol and Cambridge, and since Cambridge, John in many ways was
the senior partner in the relationship. Certainly he was the one who set
the radical pace in the Diocese. This meant that if John Robinson agreed
something with people in the Diocese it would stick, and Mervyn would
not intervene. Once David Sheppard came he was treated as a suffragan,
and the situation changed.

Canon Eric James also fell out with Mervyn soon after John left. Next
to John, Eric was the radical leader, not just in the Diocese, but in
England through the Parish And People movement which he led. Eric
went to St Albans where Bob Runcie was Bishop. Another Evangelical,
Harold Frankham, became Provost of the Cathedral in succession to the
radical Ernie Southcott. So Mervyn found himself suddenly without the
support of many of those who had brought South Bank Religion into
being. As a result he became depressed, drank too much, and listened to
some of the more Conservative Evangelical people more than he had in
the past.

The lay training team was the target for many of the Conservative
Evangelicals in the diocese. Mervyn, without John Robinson and Eric
James beside him, began to listen to their criticism. The team used
Dartmouth House for some of their training, and a committee had been
set up to run the house. This committee decided that everyone using the
house would be served vegetarian meals. Unfortunately this included
Mervyn and the ordinands who used it for retreat before ordination.
Mervyn saw himself as in charge of such an event, and was outraged
when he was told that vegetarian meals would be served to him and the
ordinands.

For Mervyn it was the last straw. He decided to take his revenge by disbanding the Council of Mission which was ultimately responsible for Dartmouth House and the lay training team. The council was to be split in two under two new boards. A clear case of divide and rule. However he needed the support of the Diocesan synod.

One of the bravest things I ever did in synod was to oppose Bishop Mervyn's motion. I did so because the Council for Mission was the most effective committee the Diocese has ever had then or since. It was totally wrong that it should be brought to an end simply because of Mervyn's annoyance at having to eat vegetarian food. I did not win of course, but a protest had been made. If John Robinson had still been Bishop of Woolwich it simply would not have happened. He would have stood up to Mervyn and won.

Shortly after this Ann and I were invited to one of Mervyn's many dinners at Bishop's House. At the end of the meal my wife and the other women present were very surprised to be asked to take coffee in another room whilst the men talked at length over port and other drinks. Mervyn must have been one of the last people in the country to get away with such misogynist behaviour. He was homosexual, though like Tony Tremlett celibate. Again after John Robinson left he did gather round him rather more homosexual clergy whom David Gerrard and I called the 'homosexual mafia'. David and I later were prominent in support of gay clergy, but there always needs to be a balance kept in any diocese, and the mafia in Southwark at this time became too powerful.

Like Tony Tremlett, Mervyn could get terribly depressed, as he admitted in his autobiography[2] that in his last five years 'he was immersed in the depths of despairing gloom.' This in both cases, was probably due to their disciplined homosexuality precluding the establishment of a permanent, sustaining relationship with a partner, which might have brought happiness and fulfilment at the deepest level. Those who insist that homosexual clergy should be celibate have a lot to answer for!

People who observed Mervyn closely became aware of strange inconsistencies. Trevor Beeson, Dean of Winchester, has rightly observed:[3]

Unmarried, he craved affection but was a demanding and sometimes ruthless friend whom it was not always easy to love. He made no secret of his socialism, but neither did he of the fact that he employed a liveried servant and a cordon bleu cook. He was genuinely concerned for the poor, and spoke up for them in the House of Lords, but he was more often in the company of the titled rich, among whom he was at various times pleased to number the Duke and Duchess of Windsor, Princess Margaret and the Prince of Wales. He hated fascism, but was a close friend of Sir Oswald Mosley who had been leader of the British fascists in the 1930s. In church matters he was the *enfant terrible* of the Establishment, which probably stood in the way of his translation to the Archbishopric of York when this fell vacant in 1975.

In spite of all this Mervyn was still a great Bishop who even in his last years was an inspiring leader. He was also far more democratic than many have realised. Senior appointments were made by the whole staff team. Names were not only suggested for the post of Archdeacon, but the staff team actually voted on who should be appointed. True Mervyn always made his position clear, but he always abided by the result. None of his successors were so democratic. We were in later years consulted, but the diocesan bishop took the decision alone.

Mervyn still encouraged the radical culture of the Diocese even if this was not as pronounced as before. One example was the appointment of Hugh Montefiore as Bishop of Kingston. As Michael de la Noy says in his biography of Mervyn[4] 'it is inconceivable that anyone other than Mervyn would have contemplated offering a Bishopric at this time to the Vicar of Great St Marys, Hugh Montefiore.' In 1967 during the course of an open lecture to the Modern Churchman's Union at Somerville College Oxford, Hugh dropped his bombshell regarding the possible sexual orientation of Christ, speculating that because he had remained unmarried, a most unusual occurrence for a Jew of his age and time, he might have been homosexual.

This did not deter Mervyn, and I remember Hugh coming before the Diocesan Conference at Church House to explain his remarks prior to his consecration as Bishop. The conference was not alarmed, but the Reverend Ian Paisley sent Hugh a telegram[5] which said, 'Bible protestants of Ulster abhor your smear on Christ and charge you with diabolical blasphemy.' Hugh framed the telegram and placed it prominently above his dining table.

I continued to attend Labour party ward meetings in Camberwell. The St Giles ward were very welcoming, partly because they knew I was not seeking any office within the party. This was a time when party members were very suspicious of middle class people like myself, because they were afraid we would take over. This eventually happened of course, but at the time middle class people would find it difficult to join the St Giles ward. Letters would go astray, information about important meetings would not be available, and in a number of ways, a small group of people kept a conservative stranglehold on the party until the early 1980s. It was the complete opposite of New Labour.

They were very good to me however. They even encouraged me to give a talk on Christianity to the ward party. They also helped when a strike looked like delaying the opening of the new St Michael's church. This would have been disastrous, as I had a number of preachers lined up, so that we opened with a bang. They included the Archbishop of Canterbury Michael Ramsey who was not the kind of person whose dates can easily be rearranged. It was a national builders strike which had been called, and there were meant to be no exceptions. However Bill Skelly, the leader of the local strikers, met me and I explained the situation. He then went and consulted his colleagues, and it was agreed that St Michael's Church would be the only site where work would be allowed to continue in the whole of the country. Later, when I came back to Southwark, Bill and I would work together on many occasions – not least when he became Mayor.

CHAPTER 7

❧✟❧

Evangelicals and Theology in the Gutter

H UGH MONTEFIORE was responsible for my next move when I became Vicar of St Luke Battersea. The churchmanship was central but one of the churchwardens held strong evangelical beliefs. He realised I was not the person to promote his vision of renewal at St Luke's. He therefore objected to my appointment. The other church-warden however was Anglo-Catholic and wished me to come. Hugh insisted that I went and the appointment was made. Today the Bishop would not have been allowed to make such an appointment, which now needs both church representatives to agree.

St Luke Battersea was a very different parish to St Michael Camberwell. I went there in 1975 when the area was beginning to be known as South Chelsea. Middle class people were moving in fast to a very desirable part of London between Clapham Common and Wandsworth Common.

The church itself is a fine red-brick basilica consecrated in 1892 and is the largest of eight churches in Battersea built by Canon Erskine Clarke. He was the Vicar of Battersea and first Vicar of St Luke's. He also built the local hospital, and was the originator of the idea that churches should publish a monthly magazine. The inside of the church is particularly beautiful with some outstanding work by the well known architect Martin Travers. Another feature are the electroliers in the nave designed from a pendant jewel by Benevenito Cellini in the Pitti Palace Florence, while those in the chancel are after paintings by Fra Angelico.

The churchwarden with strong evangelical beliefs I inherited remained for three years. He was Dr Bartley, a Consultant at St Thomas Hospital. He had a son Jonathan who sometimes played with my eldest son Andrew. He is now the Director of the Theological Think Tank Ekklesia, and writes very good articles in the *Church Times* and other newspapers. The hope must be that Evangelicals will in the future follow the moderate course that Jonathan is setting. I agreed very little with his father theologically, but he was committed to me and we were both committed to seeing St Luke's grow numerically and spiritually.

In 1975 there were about 100 people who attended sometime in a month. By the time I left ten years later this number was 400 with an average attendance of 200. This was achieved partly through a strategic plan agreed by the parochial church council soon after my arrival. Every member of the congregation was invited to join a group to advise on the way forward. What these groups said was considered at a weekend conference at Ashburnham in Sussex. We then decided to have a year of preparation in 1977 for a year of mission called 'Christianity 78' the following year. The weekend conference became a feature of life at St Luke's with as many as 200 people attending, with a programme for adults and young people.

I made every attempt to keep in touch with the twenty or so Evangelicals at St Luke's by joining their prayer group and allowing it to meet in the vicarage. This went well for six years until my wife Ann was diagnosed with a brain tumour. Luckily it was benign, and though it was the size of a golf ball, she recovered from major brain surgery, but her hearing in one ear was lost. She then had meningitis and her life was once more in danger, but again she recovered.

In the midst of all this a member of the Evangelical prayer group prayed that evil would depart the vicarage. I dread to think what would have happened if Ann had died. But this anyway was enough, and I no longer felt it was right for them to come to our home. Some of the Evangelicals left St Luke's, but most remained and were very supportive of me and my wife.

This was a difficult time. We now had three children Andrew, Sarah and Peter. To look after the children when Ann nearly died twice was difficult enough. To have one or two members of your own congregation acting as they did, and at such a time, made me very angry. I was also alarmed that mainstream charismatic Evangelical churches seemed to be encouraging a kind of Pentecostalism which is normally associated with fringe Christian groups and cults. I was aware that only some Evangelicals were charismatic, but few seemed to be criticising those Pentecostals, who are fascinated to the point of obsession with demonic spirits and the power of darkness.

This pre-occupation had been developing for some time and reached a critical point, when a previously unknown writer Frank Peretti[1] published his novel *This Present Darkness*. It sold hundreds of thousands of copies in the USA and at least 25,000 copies in the UK. The novel is about a small town in the United States of America where a battle is taking place between the demonic powers of darkness and the angelic hosts of light. The objective of both sides is to take control of the town. The hero is a devout pastor of a small fringe church. He is aided by a courageous local newspaper editor. Arrayed on the other side are the minister of a mainline church, a psychology professor and the town's chief of police. We ought to be more worried than we are that many Christians read books like this and take them seriously. They would expect the devil to be located in a Church of England vicarage.

'Christianity 78' was an opportunity to put across an intelligent Christianity both to those who went to church and, especially, those who did not. It was an outstanding success not only because of the number of people who came, but also because of those who as a result stayed and became members of the congregation. Later useful links were made with Broomwood Methodist Church nearby, and a number of events were held jointly.

In fact David Holland the minister became a great friend. Both of us had been dismayed by the decision of the Church of England not to proceed with Anglican/Methodist union. We had tried to do what we could to repair the damage at a local level. We preached regularly at each other's churches. We held some joint services, study groups and conferences. We shared a good magazine *Common News* with all the churches in South Battersea. We kept the door open for a union at a future date. This is quite important as the Methodists have relatively few Evangelicals, and unity when it comes will therefore be something of a defeat for Fundamentalists.

I did what I could to educate people in Theology. I led study groups on 'basic Christianity', and also on Hans Kung's *On Being A Christian*, a book I would still recommend to the many people in our churches who, in Kung's words, 'do not want to remain at the childhood stage in their Faith and who can no longer find any final anchorage in infallible formulas of Scripture (Protestants), of Tradition (Orthodox) or of the Magisterium (Catholics).'[2]

I enjoyed reading many books, then and later, on the New Physics and the origins of the universe. It was important Christians learnt from the truths of science, so the 'Big Bang' which created the universe and its subsequent evolution, was often a starting point for some of my sermons. Science can greatly enrich Theology by telling it what the physical universe and the world is like. However, science will never be able to prove or disprove the existence of God, nor test the origins of the universe or universes.

Professor John D. Barrow, Professor of Astronomy at Sussex University, makes this clear in his book *The Origin of the Universe*[3].

The restriction of our empirical knowledge about the Universe to the Visible Region means that we can never test the consequences of a prescription for the entire initial state of the Universe. We see only the evolutionary consequences of a tiny part of that initial state. One day we may be able to say something about the origins of our own cosmic neighbourhood. But we can never know the origins of the Universe. The deepest secrets are the ones that keep themselves.

My sermons would make it clear how much Karl Barth agreed. Barth was the Twentieth Century's greatest Theologian. He was always stressing that, with our puny minds, we can never know anything about the God who created such a Universe or Universes. The gap was just too huge. That is why God had to reveal himself to us.

Ann and I enjoyed life at St Luke's. Most of the congregation had given us wonderful support when Ann was ill and paid for a holiday when Ann was recovering. The children enjoyed the large house we then lived in. It had been built by Canon Erskine Clarke. The hall was a major feature with its grand staircase, and there was plenty of room in the four attic rooms to lay out a large scale model railway enjoyed by the children and myself. Clapham Common was close by to walk the dog and for the children to play.

The Labour Party in South Battersea arranged a dinner party for my wife and me to welcome us to the area. By the time I left St Luke's in 1985 no one at the dinner party, including myself, was still a member of the party. We were all for a time supporters of the Social Democratic Party. I never changed my views, but felt the Labour party was not the same as the one I joined in the 1960s. Later I continued to vote Labour but never rejoined the party, though Ann did for a time when we moved back to Southwark. Instead I tried to work with others to influence all political parties to take seriously the Bible's preferential option for the poor.

The growing influence of Evangelicals could be seen by two major churches in London who drew their membership from a wide area including South Battersea. Holy Trinity Brompton had about 200 people meeting in groups in Battersea, and some people from the area also attended St Mark's Kennington near the Oval. I mention these two churches because they both caused me a lot of work. People would come to me and complain about what was going on. This often happened, but let me give three examples.

A married couple were invited to a dinner party. It seemed a perfectly normal dinner party until near the end. Then it became clear that everyone present came from one of the churches mentioned, and that the dinner had been arranged solely to get the married couple to consider their brand of Evangelical Christianity. The married couple considered this appalling behaviour and I had to agree.

On another occasion a parishioner asked me to come and see her because she felt a curse had been put upon her. She told me a person had called and asked her to go to a healing service at one of these churches. When she said she did not wish to go, she was made to feel that all kinds of bad things would happen to her because she was not prepared to attend the service. In her own words she felt a curse had been put on her and she asked me to lift the curse. I prayed with her and did so.

More worrying was a fourteen year old boy who had been taken to a healing service at one of the churches. He passed out during a rather overdone laying on of hands and remained unconscious for far too long. He was eventually alright, but I did advise his parents not to go again.

In 1980 Bishop Mervyn resigned. He was given a tremendous farewell on the Wimbledon Centre Court which was packed. I still have one of the clay chalices used that day to help communicate thousands of people. He deserved the thunderous applause he got as he walked around the centre court in cope and mitre, and he enjoyed every minute.

But the Diocese needed a change and this we got with the appointment of Ronnie Bowlby. Ronnie was not a charismatic person nor was he authoritarian like Mervyn. He was scholarly, quiet, and believed in consultation and enabling others to take the lead when appropriate. Later on, when Croydon became part of the Diocese, it was decided under his leadership to have an Area system with each of the three Suffragan Bishops having some legal authority in their own area. In Mervyn's time they had been little more than Episcopal curates with the great exception of John Robinson. The change could only happen under a Bishop like Ronnie who resisted all pressures to be a Mervyn, so that the Area Bishop could act properly. Ronnie was much criticised by some who wanted to talk to the Diocesan Bishop, and hankered after the days of Mervyn and authoritarian leadership. Now they had to see their Area Bishop and take him seriously. Ronnie also appointed the first black Bishop in the Church of England, when he made Wilfred Wood Bishop of Croydon.

In 1981 I was appointed Rural Dean of Battersea. This was a post I held as well as continuing to be Vicar of St Luke's. It meant chairing the Deanery Synod and its standing committee, as well as having oversight of the churches, clergy and people of Battersea. I also became chair of Wandsworth Welcare. We employed three social workers to work with parents and children in the Borough of Wandsworth. This was important Christian social work which the Church had done for some time.

The 1980s were a turning point. As Borough social work began to decline, there was an opportunity for the Church to do more, and eventually to win contracts for work previously done by Social Services. To take full advantage of this the Welcares in the Diocese, which were all independent charities, needed to work together more. This is now happening, and many new areas of work have started, and more are possible.

Two people were very important to me at this time. The first was Dr Cecilia Goodenough. Cecilia was a powerful woman and an admiral's daughter. She was very anti-clerical and was said to eat several curates for breakfast. She thought it disgraceful that women should want to demean themselves by being ordained. We had first met in the early 1970s when I was Vicar of St Michael Camberwell. I joined a bible study group which she led as Diocesan Lay Missioner and was chaired by Canon Gordon Davies. At every meeting Cecilia and I argued. After six weeks, other members of the group got alarmed and wondered if I was alright, as Cecilia could be very hard hitting. But we both respected each other and indeed enjoyed each other's company. I sat at her feet for many years.

The second person was Canon Ivor Smith-Cameron. He came to the Diocese as Canon Missioner after Eric James resigned. He teamed up with Cecilia in a house in Clapham not far from my vicarage in Battersea. Cecilia continued to run her bible study group from Ivor's house. It became something of a haven for liberal Christians who wished to study the bible in an intelligent way.

The group thinking that was done at 25 The Chase Clapham was summed up by Cecilia in *Theology in the Gutter*.[4] These studies she reminded us did not emerge from high places or learned situations. Those of us who were involved in them are 'gutter people'. We do theology from where we are, however unpromising our standing place may be. It is where we belong. We follow Ezekiel in Chapter 3 verse 15 when he says, 'I sat where they sat and stayed there.'

Throughout these studies we attempted in our thinking to keep close to biblical insights and to give them free reign in illuminating our thinking. But this was never done in isolation. On a number of occasions we based our study and discussion on the content of some contemporary book (fact or fiction) which offered insights on a matter of importance to our contemporary living. The primary objective of these studies was Mission understood in its widest sense; not simply as an endeavour to bring our public to some form of Christian commitment; but rather together to explore as deeply as we could our understanding of life with God; the meaning of our common humanity and the insights which are available to us in these areas through a growing an open-minded reflection on the Scriptures both Old and New Testament and the life and proclamation of Christ.

Cecilia was very anxious that our study of academic theology should lead us to having something to say to the living. She told a story about a friend of hers who lived in Battersea:[5]

'She had a hard life, and of that there was no doubt,' she said. 'She had a husband who was a rather singular character who was in and out of prison. She didn't mind that so much and got accustomed to it ... She had seven children – six riotous boys and a miserable downtrodden little girl who was at everyone's beck and call. I went to the Vicar of the parish in which this woman lived and suggested "I am not asking you to go yourself, but perhaps someone in your congregation might go and just see if there was any line of friendship;" and so he agreed reluctantly and I left. A little while later I went to see her, and we were chatting in the kitchen and I say "By the way, did anyone come from the church?" "Yes." "Well you don't sound very jolly about it, what happened?" "Well, you know how it is, he came but he didn't seem to have nothing to say." I knew just what she meant. It wasn't that she wanted him to have anything to say about religion, but he hadn't anything to say about anything that had to do with her life, and this is what I mean when I say that we are not engaged in study on a purely intellectual exercise. We are here to engage together as people.'

The Diocesan Council for Social Aid was one area where Cecilia and I worked together. When I first joined in the late 1960s it was the Southwark Diocesan Church of England Temperance Society. It ran Ellison House, an approved hostel for young men between the ages of seventeen and nineteen. I was joint Chaplain with the Reverend Jack Pawsey. My friends were much amused that I had anything to do with the Temperance Society. But the name was soon changed to the Diocesan Council For Social Aid. A new probation hostel for young men was planned. Ellison House would be sold and the money released for other work.

This enabled the Council For Social Aid in 1970 to sponsor an enquiry into the needs for Social Aid in South London. A working party was convened, chaired by Canon Eric James and with Cecilia Goodenough as a member. The result of the enquiry was that Social Aid should concentrate on four areas of work. These were Race Relations, Community Development, the Single Homeless and Ellison House. Four sub-committees were therefore set up to manage the work and appoint workers to aid the committees in their actions. I was involved in two of these committees.

First I chaired the Ellison House management committee until I left Camberwell in 1975. A new probation hostel was built at the request of the Home Office, not for young men, but for adult male offenders aged between 25 and 35 years. Dr Pat Logan acted as secretary of the hostel as well as working with the Single Homeless Group.

Secondly, I chaired the Community Development Group until 1986. As vicar of St Michael Camberwell I had worked closely with the Local Community Development worker Gerry Williams. He joined the group and gave us helpful advice. We eventually appointed John Richards as the first Diocesan Community Worker to encourage and enable community work in the parishes of the Diocese, especially in the inner city. As a result, a number of parishes have appointed their own Community Workers over the years, or have worked closely with those already in their areas. The Church is ideally placed to help as it uniquely has a local building which can be used by the community, local people on the ground who go to church in that building, and a professional clergy person who lives in the area rather than commuting in from outside.

The Social Aid Committee also employed the first Race Relations Worker in the Diocese who was Jack Pawsey. But it soon became clear that a black worker was required, and under the guidance of Wilfred Wood, the first black Bishop of Croydon, a team of three black people were employed to do this important work. Eventually I chaired the Executive Committee of The Council for Social Aid, but gave this up shortly before becoming Archdeacon.

I still enjoyed being Vicar of St Luke's and Rural Dean of Battersea. I particularly looked forward to the annual week long St Luke's Festival. 'Any Questions' was broadcast live by the BBC. The opening Festival Eucharist was also televised by ITV. *Songs of Praise* was broadcast from St Luke's on BBC TV. But equally exciting were the plays put on by members of the parish and the music performed by our own Festival Chorus. Local actors like Timothy West and Prunella Scales took part, and many other community events for families and children were organised.

It was therefore with mixed feelings I learned in 1985 that I had been appointed Archdeacon of Southwark. We were not able to move till May 1986, which gave us time to have one more Christmas in the grandeur of St Luke's vicarage. We invited 30 members of the family for Christmas dinner because there was room for them all to dine in the large hall at the bottom of the grand staircase.

The children were not too pleased at first about the move, but soon got used to the rather smaller house in Dog Kennel Hill, East Dulwich, where the Archdeacon of Southwark lived. It helped that no one had to change school as Westminster City School and Greycoat Hospital School were as easy to get to from Southwark as Battersea. They were both comprehensive schools in Westminster but also Church of England foundations. Nevertheless it was not easy for our children to reply to the question, What is your name? What does your father do? Now in addition when asked, 'Where do you live?' they had to answer, ' Dog Kennel Hill!'

CHAPTER 8

❧✝❧

Faith in the City

THE office of Archdeacon is an ancient one going back over 1,000 years. Archdeacons were particularly important in medieval times when, during their Visitation of an area, people who had committed offences were brought before the Archdeacon in his church court. Many of the offences were of a sexual nature which is why it was called the 'Bawdy Court' rather than the correct 'Archdeacons Court'.

In the eighteenth century Archdeacons ran most dioceses. The Bishop would remain at Westminster doing his duty in the House of Lords. He would visit his Diocese when Parliament broke up for the summer holidays, and mass confirmations would be arranged.

Today the job of an Archdeacon is just as important. He works with the Bishop to manage the Diocese. He is a member of the Bishop's staff meeting. He is particularly responsible for property, finance and administration, and sits on all the Diocesan committees which deal with these matters. He is a pastor to the clergy, especially the Churchwardens in the churches of his Archdeaconry. He inspects these churches each year and Churchwardens must answer questions in the Articles Of Enquiry which he sends to them. All Churchwardens have to be sworn into office by the Archdeacon and listen to his Charge. He no longer has a court, but he still has legal powers and responsibilities, which only he can carry out. He can act as a Judge in minor ecclesiastical planning matters, and he has an important role to play in major ones.

I was not just appointed Archdeacon of Southwark but also 'Faith in the City Officer' for the whole Diocese with the job of implementing the report when it came out. The Archbishop of Canterbury Robert Runcie had set up a Commission chaired by Sir Richard O'Brien the former chair of the Manpower Services Commission, to examine the strengths, insights, problems and needs of the Church's life and mission in the inner city, and to reflect on the challenge which God may be making to the Church and Nation. Its members included academics, theologians, social workers, a head teacher, a trade union leader, clergy, laity and a significant black presence. It was the idea of Canon Eric James who helped to facilitate the Commission, as did a civil servant John Pearson seconded from the Department of the Environment.

The report[1] found 'a grave and fundamental injustice in the Urban Priority Areas' and it commented on the sense of alienation of those who lived in them, particularly the young, and of the devastating impact of 'unemployment, decayed housing, sub-standard educational and medical provisions and social disintegration.' The Commission recommended, among 38 other suggestions, that the Church of England set up a Church Urban Fund to finance appropriate projects in the inner cities. It made 23 recommendations to government on themes like job creation, increased child benefit, positive measures against racial discrimination in employment and housing, the raising of the rate support grant, and an inquiry into mortgage tax relief which worked solely to the advantage of the better off.

Immediately on its appearance in 1985, the report was condemned by Conservative MPs including a Cabinet Minister who called it Marxist. It was attacked by the Tory press which resulted in best-selling sales of the report, warm support from a number of distinguished and knowledgeable people, and the support of the *Financial Times*. It was an exciting time, especially as it seemed to many commentators to offer a more telling and radical indictment of the Conservative Government than any document produced by the Official Opposition Parties.

Mrs Thatcher was certainly livid. For a time she would go out of her way to handbag anyone who had anything to do with the writing of the report. This Canon Eric James found when he was present with her at a social gathering. She immediately engaged him in an animated and fairly one-sided conversation.

The expertise evident in the report was to have far-reaching results, not only in stimulating Government action, but also in the raising of over £30 million from charitable trusts, business and by churchgoers themselves, to create the Church Urban Fund which would enable inner city projects over twenty years. The Fund awarded £4.5 million to 365 community projects in Southwark Diocese and this helped to bring in a further £30,000,000 from other sources. This was due to the work of three people I helped to appoint. Steph Blackwell was made the Diocesan Church Urban Fund Adviser, and she worked closely with the Diocesan Community Work Advisers Ann Stricklen and Jill McKinnon who followed John Richards in the post.

It was a landmark moment. Local councils, trade unions and other institutions who had been very critical of the Church were strongly in favour of the report. Greenwich Council, which had previously passed a resolution banning its Mayor from attending the Institution of Vicars, immediately organised its own *Faith in the City* conference. Other Borough Councils followed, including Southwark, which held three such conferences over ten years. Ron Keating spoke at the first conference. He was Assistant General Secretary of the National Union of Public Employees as well as a member of the Archbishop's Commission. I remember him explaining to surprised Labour councillors in Southwark that the Church had far more people on the ground in inner city areas than they had. Michael Heseltine addressing the National Conference of *Faith in the City* officers urged the church not to be afraid to speak out if a real impact was to be made.

My own experience was that the Church was a much more credible force after 1985. I encouraged and helped to organise a large number of *Faith in the City* conferences throughout the Diocese and beyond. I found that many politicians who had not taken the Church seriously before, did so now. I took advantage of this new situation to form new partnerships. I had regular meetings with the Chief Executive of Southwark Borough Council and I encouraged my fellow Archdeacons and Borough Deans to do the same throughout the Diocese. We got to know the politicians of all parties better, and gradually the Church came to be consulted more and to be a partner in making things better. A good example was housing.

The *Faith in the City* report made clear that a 'home is more than bricks and mortar, more than a roof over one's head. Decent housing certainly means a place that is dry, warm and in reasonable repair. It also means security, privacy, sufficient space; a place where people can grow, make choices, become more whole people. It also relates to the environment in which the house is located as much as the condition inside the front door. Vandalism, graffiti, fear of violence, lack of play space, all affect how people regard their surroundings. How property is managed, as well as its physical condition, is important for it affects how people make decisions. To believe that you have no control over one of the most basic areas of your life is to feel devalued.'[2]

And yet thousands of people in Southwark were forced to live in massive and inhuman concrete jungles, described by a tenant in the *Faith in the City* report as 'living in a mistake'[3]! It is monstrous that people should be made to live in badly designed and often badly managed mistakes – especially as the mistake was not made by them but by Labour and Conservative politicians acting on the advice of the Department of the Environment housing staff, who made available subsidies and regulations that dragooned local authorities into accepting these Corbusian policies.

So the Church did what it could to rectify this situation following the 1985 report. Together with the Council Leader and local tenants, I arranged for the Bishop of Southwark, Ronnie Bowlby, to meet with the Housing Minister on the North Peckham and Gloucester Grove estates. We walked the Minister round the estates, and then the Bishop chaired a meeting at which the Minister was questioned about what the Government could do to help. Subsequently the Bishop of Woolwich Peter Hall and myself had a meeting with Kenneth Clarke and the civil servants in charge of the government of London. The GLC had been abolished. Eventually it was accepted that most of the estates should come down and better homes be built in consultation with local people including the Church.

We were also involved in building some of those new homes. The Diocesan Housing Association, which I chaired, built some of the new housing to show the people of Peckham that we considered the area a priority. A mix of housing was built and the area today is transformed.

But the story did not end there, for I was constantly reminding Local and Central Government that they needed to rediscover housing management as taught by that great Christian Octavia Hill. She built hundreds of houses for poor people in Southwark one hundred years ago, and we needed to relearn her management skills. That was not just my view, but that of Anne Power[4] in her important book *Property Before People, The Management Of Twentieth Century Council Housing*. Anne found that the problems she and others were facing in the Priority Estates Project in the 1980s were strikingly similar to those faced by Octavia Hill and her housing managers (who were all women). So they began to look again at her remedies which, though simple, had been completely forgotten by those in council house management (mostly men) in the last sixty years. Octavia Hill's remedies were:

Repair houses incrementally and constantly, in line with tenant preferences and in proportion to their support for the improvements; do not displace existing tenants, help the most needy; give housing jobs to residents; collect rents personally door to door weekly [eviction though accepted as a last resort, was rarely used]; put one manager in charge of a small area of not more than 300 households and responsible for every aspect of dealing with tenants; link social and housing needs, business and personal support; give tenants maximum say and responsibility for their housing; be tough minded and assertive with those who make other people's lives miserable.

In urging this kind of housing management in Southwark it was helpful to be able to point to the 800 tenancy Octavia Hill estate in Southwark which was then still managed by the Church Commissioners, as it was in Octavia's day. Gradually the Borough council came to see the importance of good management and implemented some of Octavia Hill's and Anne Power's remedies.

I have already mentioned the role played by Ron Keating as a special speaker at *Faith in the City* conferences. He was a Christian trade union leader at the headquarters of his union the National Union of Public Employees, which was in the Diocese. He agreed to my invitation to chair a group of people from Urban Priority Areas whom I had drawn together to encourage others from the inner-city to play a greater role in the Church. This resulted in a yearly conference of people from Urban Priority Area parishes to enable the voice of inner-city people to be heard.

Later at the initiation of Dr Peter Selby the Bishop of Kingston a Black Forum was also launched for similar reasons. The Forum's declared aim was to provide 'opportunities for the voices and views of black and minority ethnic members of the Church throughout Southwark Diocese to be freely expressed on any matter of concern, interest and importance to them, and to enable them to articulate their perceptions, affirm their worship, faith and culture as active members of the family of God.'

One of the first things I did when made Archdeacon of Southwark in 1985 was to contact Councillor Sam King who was the first black Mayor of Southwark. He served in the RAF during the war and came to Britain on the Empire Windrush which landed at Tilbury, bringing the first Jamaican settlers to Britain. We immediately struck up a friendship and worked together in various ways for the next eighteen years.

I persuaded him to put himself forward as the Black Led Church's Borough Dean, for up to that point these churches were not represented at the regular meetings of Ecumenical Borough Deans in Southwark. The Deans were the chosen representatives of each denomination for working together on social responsibility issues, and in particular for liaising with the Borough Council. Sam called a meeting of the Black Led Churches and they agreed he should represent them.

This was very important, not only because it brought the Black Led Churches on board, but also because Sam was a much respected

Councillor and his voice would be listened to. It considerably strengthened our hand when we met with Councillors and Officers to prepare for the three *Faith in the City* conferences which were held in Southwark. The Borough Deans and Officers also met afterward to ensure the implementation of what we agreed and to monitor progress.

At first, as the Anglican Borough Dean I met with the Chief Executive Anna Wyatt on my own and reported back to the other Borough Deans. Eventually it was agreed that all the Borough Deans would meet with the Chief Executive and the Leader of the Council. This took time to arrange, but the new climate generated by the *Faith in the City* report eventually made it possible.

Before each meeting the Borough Deans would agree the agenda items we wished to discuss when we met the Leader and Chief Executive. They would add their own items to the agenda and make sure the lead officer was present for the items we discussed. In this way the Borough Deans were able to bring considerable influence to bear on all matters Local Government dealt with.

I also represented the Diocesan Board of Education on the Borough Education Committee. The Church of England and Roman Catholic Church legally have to be on such committees if there are church schools in a Borough, and we also have a vote. This was particularly important in Southwark where 50% of children attended Church schools. I got on very well with the Roman Catholic representative and we worked together for the benefit of all schools in the Borough. There was even a period of two years when there was a hung council and our two votes were crucial. We were obviously listened to very carefully then, but even when our votes could not sway the result, we still had considerable influence. This was surely right, especially as the best schools were nearly always Church schools.

The introduction of Cabinet Government relegated us to the much weaker Overview and Scrutiny Committee of the Council. However we were still members of the genuinely powerful Schools Organisation Committee which did not have to be chaired by a Councillor. I was elected chair of this important committee where decisions are taken, previously reserved to the Secretary of State, about closing, opening or expanding schools, and to which the Education Cabinet Minister is answerable.

The partnership between the Church and Southwark Borough Council grew gradually stronger over the years. In 1985 there were very few Christian Councillors and many Councillors were suspicious of the

Church. As a result of *Faith in the City* many more Christians became Councillors. By the 1990s a large number of Councillors in Southwark were active Christians. By 2000 it was usual for the leader and some Cabinet Members to be Christian and for many Councillors to be Anglican. This meant that a very different culture prevailed, with Councillors willingly working with the Church to regenerate the inner city for the good of the people of Southwark.

A good example of this was seen following the murder of Damilola Taylor on a part of the North Peckham estate before it was demolished. The Church took the lead over the services which were held both at the time, and a year later, when I encouraged the Archbishop of Canterbury George Carey to take part in a service to mark the opening of the Damilola Taylor centre. His visit was very much appreciated by Damilola's parents. There was a march from the town hall to St Luke's church in Peckham which went past Damilola's school and the site of the murder. The march was led by Members of Parliament, councillors, the Bishop of Woolwich, myself and other church leaders. It was important however to do more, and so the Borough Deans met with the Leader and Chief Executive to see what could be done to prevent young children of twelve and under being involved in gangs on the streets. It was agreed that the Borough Deans and Council Officers would call together all those working with young people in Peckham to look at the situation and see how it could be improved. The police, clergy, youth workers and youth offending team were all invited. The meetings were a great success and they were organised by the Ichthus Borough Dean Simon Thomas. They discovered that there were an amazing number of voluntary bodies already working in the area, but they did not know what everybody else was doing. Now they knew, and could therefore help one another to be more effective. They could also work more closely with the youth offending team, the police and the schools. A year later the situation had considerably improved.

I had always seen the need for expert help for myself when I acted as Borough Dean. From 1986 onwards therefore I set up my own Think Tank. I invited people with expertise in different areas. We met six times a year over lunch and I shared with them the problems of the Borough, seeking their guidance on the role the Church ought to play, and in particular what the Borough Deans should raise at our meetings with the Chief Executive and Leader of the Council.

One of the recommendations which the first *Faith in the City* conference in the Borough made was that church land should be used for affordable housing. Bishop Ronnie Bowlby asked me to arrange for the existing Diocesan Housing Association to do this. I had never heard of it. The reason was that although it had been started by Bishop John Robinson in the late 1960s, nothing had happened since and it was moribund. It was not even a registered housing association.

I therefore sought to get it registered with the housing corporation. This took a long time to achieve because small housing associations are thought by many not to be a good idea. We asked to be registered so that we could build mainly on church land which might be sold to us by the Diocese at less than market value.

Eventually we got going and I chaired the housing association for over ten years. We employed two very good Directors, Giles Goddard who got us going, and Steve Joyce who built on what Giles did and expanded it. Some housing was built in North Peckham as already mentioned. In two cases new housing was built on the site of a large Victorian church, but we also built a new church and church hall on the same site. After ten years the London diocese joined us and we became the Southwark and London Diocesan Housing Association. We were then able to build affordable housing on any church site which was available for redevelopment across London. Four staff are now employed and many new developments of housing are being built.

I spoke at a number of conferences, some in the Diocese but sometimes elsewhere. Perhaps the most important was the address I gave in June 1988 to the Association of Metropolitan Authorities at their headquarters in Westminster. This account of the conference in the *Guardian* on the 8th June summaries what I said: [5]

CLERIC CRITICISES INNER-CITY POLICY
'DISASTER RECIPE'

'The Government's inner city policy was a recipe for disaster', the Archdeacon of Southwark, the Venerable Douglas Bartles-Smith said yesterday.

Only sensitive policing had prevented more trouble on the scale of the Brixton riots, he told a seminar in London.

'All the churches are deeply worried. I don't think the government recognises there is a connection between wealth obsession and social ills associated with family break up, drug taking and homelessness.'

He said later that Mrs Thatcher's recent 'sermon' on Christian morality opened the door to more church pressure because she conceded the point that moral and theological issues had a part to play.

The Archdeacon, representing the Archbishop of Canterbury's Faith in the City Committee, told the Association of Metropolitan Authorities that the situation had worsened. The rich had been made richer and the poor poorer. There was no sign of money trickling down to urban priority areas.

'The government is intent on imposing top down solutions to the problems of the inner city without really listening to anybody except the private sector. So we have the ridiculous situation of those who do not live in it not listening to those who live and work there. This is a recipe for disaster.'

In 1990 the Bishop of Southwark Ronnie Bowlby asked me to go to one of the earliest performances of David Hare's new play *Racing Demon* at the National Theatre. He was worried David might have got hold of some recent scandal when talking to priests in the Southwark Diocese during his research. It was known that David had spent most of 1987 and 1988 preparing to write the play.

David did this at a time when the tensions in the Church of England were revealed for all to see. In December 1987 an Oxford don named Gareth Bennett killed himself after having been identified as the anonymous author of Crockford's preface, critical of the liberal hierarchy in the Church of England. 'There was, for those of us who had been following the Church's affairs,' said David Hare in his book[6] *Asking Around,* 'an unpleasant sense of the inevitable. Even as distant and recent an observer as myself had realised that, underneath the polite Christian surface, passionate positions were being taken up in the Church which simply could not be reconciled. The Church could no longer be all things to all men. When Bennett murdered his cat, then climbed into his car and fixed a rubber hosepipe to his exhaust, he was offering the Church a death which would be interpreted by his friends as a kind of martyrdom, and by his enemies as the worst and dirtiest kind of suicide: the kind which is intended to upset everybody.'

David Hare had been to the General Synod, he had talked to Eric James, the Reverend Tony Higton and Charles Moore, but above all he had talked to four inner city priests in the Southwark diocese, some of whom were in a Team Ministry. David puts it like this in *Asking Around:*[7]

Some months later I was to attend a session of Synod at which the Archbishop of Canterbury had to endure the humiliating ordeal of sitting silent while 400 delegates discussed the degree to which he was or wasn't personally responsible for Gareth Bennett's death. But by then it had already become clear to me that my true interests lay not with the bishops, nor indeed with the kind of priests who relish the politics of synod, but with those people who give up their lives to minister in the inner cities. I was interested to discover the attitudes sustaining them in what might appear to be the thankless task of interesting the local population in Jesus Christ . . . . The more I interviewed priests and parishioners in that amorphous area of South London which runs between the Elephant and Castle and Streatham High Road, the more aware I was of the anxieties the team principle had created. But at the same time I never lost my conviction that on £8,000 per annum, loving God and trying to clear up society's worst problems, here were some heroes for our age.

The play was partly based on an incident in the Lambeth Team Ministry, when Bishop Mervyn Stockwood had acted very badly in getting rid of the Rector Richard Moberley,[8] whose likeness to Lionel in the play is very clear. Richard was aware that Mervyn disapproved of Team Ministries, and wished to appoint one of his protégés to the Team Rectorship. When Richard went to see him and told him that the Bishop of Kingston had implied his tenure would be renewed, Mervyn lost his temper and said, 'He has no right. I make the appointments. I have taken legal advice and you have no security of tenure.' He then offered Richard a job in Thamesmead. The Archdeacon came to see Richard and re-iterated Mervyn's view. Richard wondered what would happen if he took his own legal advice. The Archdeacon said, 'I can tell you what will happen. You will never get a job in the Church of England again.'[9]

This was used by David Hare as the main plot of the play. He disguised it a little by making the Bishop of Southwark hold views similar to those of the then Bishop of London, who was against the ordination of women to the priesthood. There was however nothing about more recent times to worry Ronnie Bowlby. Indeed quite the opposite, for it is a very good play, perhaps David Hare's best, and he was quite justified in making Southwark's inner city priests the heroes. For in my experience that is what they were!

The official summary of the play said, 'In conflict with the government, torn with internal dissension on matters of doctrine and practice, the Church of England finds itself enjoying unwelcome publicity. Many of the church's tensions come into relief in this story of four priests in South London who are struggling in moving and often hilarious ways to make sense of their mission in the inner city.'

David Hare makes it clear that 'some of my original interest in the inner city churches had come about from my reading of the famous Church of England report *Faith in the City*. I admit I was attracted more by the sympathetic loneliness of its clergy than by its sometimes infuriating theology.'[10]

For many people the best moment in *Racing Demon*[11] comes when

the Reverend Streaky Bacon enters the church late at night to pray –
having drunk more than he should with the Bishop of Southwark (an
occupational hazard in those days).

Lord, I have no theology. Can't do it. By my bed, there's a pile of paperbacks
called *The Meaning of Meaning* and *How to Ask Why?* They've been there for
years. The whole thing's so clear. You're there. In people's happiness. Tonight,
in the taste of that drink. Or the love of my friends. The whole thing's so
simple. Infinitely loving.
    Why do people find it so hard?

There were at least three reasons for the increased tensions in the
Church in the 1980s. First the debate about the ordination of women to
the priesthood was hotting up, and traditional Catholics like Gareth
Bennett were getting very worried. Second the Conservative Evangelicals were continuing to grow in strength and for the first time made
a real impact in synod. Tony Higton put down a motion calling for
the reaffirmation of biblical standards of morality, condemning forni-
cation, adultery and homosexual acts in all circumstances, and demanding of Christian leaders that they should be 'exemplary' in all spheres of
morality.

This had been precipitated partly by the third reason, which was the
appointment of David Jenkins as Bishop of Durham. In the course of a
television interview he expressed doubts concerning the historical
veracity of the virgin birth and the physical Resurrection of Jesus. A
storm of protest arose and he was accused by Evangelicals of denying the
Christian faith.

The trouble was that the Conservative Evangelicals, previously stuck
in their own ghetto, had not known what the Church of England was
really like. The Evangelical world where no one had doubts, or at least
never expressed them, was not typical of the rest of the Church of
England. Similarly, because gay Evangelicals kept quiet, they had no idea
that there were lots of good priests, especially in the inner cities, who
were gay and lived with their partners. In 1987 Tony Higton had most of
the media on his side and Mrs Thatcher's government soon introduced
Clause 28. This effectively prevented councils from spending money on
projects, including advice services, which could be alleged to make gay
life styles somehow more attractive.

All this saddened me a great deal. I liked the Bishop of Durham. He
was not saying anything which was not already discussed in theological
colleges or universities. He believed strongly in the Resurrection and was

able to get people to discuss the subject in pubs at Easter time. I also found it shocking that Anglicans discriminated against women and gay people, and that Anglican Bishops failed to lead the human rights agenda, leaving Christianity to emerge too slowly from medievalism. People in London, outside the Church, were also shocked because equal opportunities were expected by everybody. After a few years the views of the people of England changed nearer to that of the people of London. Soon most people would be appalled at the Church's position.

The Church of England was changing but in the wrong direction. The Evangelicals were beginning to dominate the church. I soon found myself working for three of them. George Carey became Archbishop of Canterbury, Roy Williamson Bishop of Southwark and Peter Hall was already Bishop of Woolwich. They were all moderate Evangelicals, but Roy Williamson and Peter Hall were much more acceptable than George Carey.

Roy Williamson was an Ulsterman born into a Belfast family of fourteen children. He had previously been Bishop of Bradford. He arrived to discover that Southwark's Area system introduced by Ronnie Bowlby had in some respects written him out of a role. He responded, not by seeking to claw back any of the authority which his predecessor had delegated, but by developing new forms of episcopal activity. He was a good communicator and he listened. He especially listened to the many gay clergy in the Diocese and encouraged them. They responded by being open with him, and they trusted him.

Peter Hall was the inner city Bishop as well as being the Bishop of Woolwich. I worked with him very closely. He was also very supportive of gay clergy in his area. He was an Evangelical who strongly advocated the Social Gospel, and was so liberal that he was not seen as an Evangelical by many in the Diocese. Southwark under new management was not quite as radical as it had been, but it was still more radical than any other Diocese.

George Carey was quite different, Though moderate, he was a real Evangelical. He seemed more interested in the Decade of Evangelism, which failed to increase church attendance, than in standing up for the inner cities. He came to the *Faith in the City* Officers National Conference where he was poorly received. He tried to suggest to the conference that the Church did not speak with special expertise in political and economic matters. Everyone was infuriated that he said this to a conference which included the Anglican economist Will Hutton amongst others. I was so appalled that I sent this letter to the Church of England Newspaper which published it as the first letter:

DR CAREY LETS THE INNER CITIES DOWN [12]

Sir, The Archbishop of Canterbury greatly angered most of those who attended the National Faith in the City conference when he said that ... 'when it comes to the most effective political and economic means of attaining desirable moral goals, the churches ... do not speak with special expertise.' The Archbishop seemed to be unaware of the considerable and mainly lay expertise of those attending the conference – many of whom felt insulted by his remarks.

Dr Carey needs to follow the example of his predecessor and use this 'expertise' himself more in the future. It was left to Will Hutton, an Anglican economist and editor of the *Observer*, to compliment those attending the conference on what had been achieved and to urge the Church to speak out more.'

The Bishops under Dr Carey's leadership said nothing during the 1992 Election. This was in stark contrast to 1987 when they spoke out strongly on inner city issues. It was therefore left to me to call together ten *Faith in the City* officers, and we wrote a letter to *The Times* which was published as the lead letter of the day under my name on 26th March 1992, shortly before the election. It caused quite a stir:

URBAN DECAY AS PARTY PRIORITY
FROM THE ARCHDEACON OF SOUTHWARK AND OTHERS [13]

Sir, We have been appointed by our respective dioceses to monitor the way the Church and our society have responded to the detailed recommendations of the Church of England's *Faith in the City* report. That report defined 1,122 parishes as 'urban priority areas' (UPAs), each of them characterised by economic decline, physical decay and social disintegration.

We wish to place on record that, whilst the church has responded in many remarkable ways to the needs of people living in UPAs, the overall situation within them has deteriorated in the past seven years.

Economic decline has deepened; long term unemployment has risen; the numbers in or on the margins of poverty has risen; the value of benefits have fallen, especially for those under 25. Physical decay has worsened: whether it be the state of our schools and hospitals and housing stock, or the conditions of roads, parks, open spaces and libraries, the overwhelming experience is one of grievous neglect.

Social disintegration has escalated and is everywhere apparent – in the periodic urban eruptions; in the huge increase in crime especially in crimes of violence; in the prevalence of child abuse and domestic violence; in the crumbling services on which people depend, such as law and advice centres; and supremely in the massive rise of homelessness across the country. On almost every conceivable index, people in UPAs are in a worse situation than they were in 1985.

At a more profound level, however, we wish to declare our deep conviction that this deterioration testifies to a bankrupt social vision which has guided our economic and social policy over the past decade. As we approach the election, we need to acknowledge and reassert the moral and ethical basis of our institutions and to go beyond the destructive individualism which has so corroded our sense of shared humanity and common destiny.

Unless this ethical and ultimately spiritual dimension is addressed by each of the political parties, then no amount of tinkering with our institutions, multiplying choices or increasing resources, will address the needs of those living in the UPAs of our land. There must be more to life than shopping and television and all the political parties have a duty to spell out what their social vision is, how it will resolve the grave social injustice which continues to mar our country and how it will unify its people in a common social hope.

This did have a surprising impact and resulted in considerable debate on inner city issues a week before the election. But why had the Bishops failed to speak out? They had certainly been urged to do so. There was little doubt however that George Carey's appointment had been partly brought about by Margaret Thatcher. She had appointed Viscount Caldecote, a leading lay Evangelical, as the chair of the Crown Appointments Commission. Another Evangelical, her Appointments Secretary Robin Catford, was also a secretary to the Commission.

I was convinced the new Archbishop was already having an inhibiting effect on the Bishops. I therefore took the matter to the next National Conference where I argued we needed to do better in the future. A prophetic Christianity could make a difference as the *Faith in the City* report had shown. We must keep the pressure on government.

This was the theme of my new book *Opportunities For A Strong Church* which was published in December 1993. The reviews summarise quite well what I wrote:[14]

The media myth of a Church in hopeless decline must be shown to be false, peddled by the ignorant and those who do not like the impact the Church has undoubtedly made in the 1980s ... Many people express a belief in God even if they don't attend church regularly. A large proportion of people turn to the Church for recognised rites of passage – baptisms, weddings and funerals.

Because the Church is at the heart of society in a way which would not be possible if it were disestablished, it has the opportunity for influence at the highest level .... The fall of Communism and the end of socialism gives the

Church of England a rare opportunity to further extend the influence of Christianity. There is a need to ask penetrating questions of an over mighty and triumphant capitalism; and also to remind the one party government of this country that, although elected by a permanent affluent majority, they must nevertheless govern for the good of all, according to biblical insights.

The Church therefore, says the author, must become the opposition, and speak out for the poor, the weak and those marginalized in our society . . . We must have a vision similar to that enjoyed by Moses and the Israelite leaders as they prepared to enter the Promised Land. God has spoken to us through the burning bush of inner-city riots on more than one occasion in recent years and we ignore the call to action at our peril.

The book also had an important chapter on the need for tolerance. In 1990 the secular magazine *New Woman*[15] conducted a survey which said that 61% of those who were questioned felt that rather than creating a 'family of man' the Church creates bigots and divides nations. 75% felt that the Church had a role to play in today's world, but more than half said it is playing the wrong role. The vast majority believed that the Church should stay out of people's personal lives. The actions of Archbishop Desmond Tutu and Terry Waite were generally applauded as being the kind of role the Church should play.

These results are very similar to the European Values group survey[16] which found that most Europeans believed Churches should speak out more on subjects like the third world, racial discrimination and ecology, but should say less about abortion, extra-marital affairs, euthanasia and homosexuality.

Clearly many people are fed up with a growing religious intolerance and fundamentalism. Many would share the anger of the novelist A. N. Wilson when he wrote[17],

We cannot stop the Pope appearing on his balcony and telling us how to think and behave, any more than we stop 'fatwas' being issued from the Ayatollah. But we can do more than turn a deaf ear to them when they do so. We can cheer when their own people have the spirit to rebel against them, and we can boo whenever these religious bullies open their mouths. It is true that they are frightening, particularly when they issue threats of death. But it is a definition of cowardice that we should feel frightened of saying boo to a goose. The Pope is a very powerful goose. The Ayatollah Khameini is an even greater goose. Mrs Whitehouse is a minor goose. The Reverend Tony Higton and Ian Paisley are noisy little ganders. Boo, boo, boo to them all.

The religious intolerance that so many people dislike is more often found outside the Church of England. The Reverend Ian Paisley does a great deal of damage, and Northern Ireland was frequently mentioned by those in the survey who felt the Churches create bigots and divide nations. The Roman Catholic position on contraception has been criticised by many Anglicans including the Archbishop of Canterbury. Nevertheless in recent years intolerance has begun to rear its ugly head in the Church of England. Evangelicals like Tony Higton were putting pressure on Bishops not to allow gay priests to have partners.

As the decade wore on, moderate Evangelicals gave way to fundamentalist Evangelicals. Homophobia and sexism in the Church got worse rather than better. The Archbishop of Canterbury George Carey was siding with his fellow Conservative Evangelicals. In April 1997 he ruled out a Church Blessing for gay people. I had had enough of such bigotry so I wrote the following letter which was published in *The Times*:

GAY 'MARRIAGES' [18]
FROM THE ARCHDEACON OF SOUTHWARK

Sir, Archbishops of Canterbury (like Popes) should be ignored when they talk about sex ('Carey rules out Church Blessing for gay marriage' April 16). Why should homosexual priests be celibate when heterosexual priests like the Archbishop and myself are not? Could the Archbishop have remained celibate if he were refused the option of marriage?

I could not and would not, therefore, enforce celibacy on anyone.'

I had told Bishop Roy Williamson about this letter before it was published and he supported my right to do so, even though some protested and one Anglican priest left for Rome.

Meanwhile women priests had been ordained after a long and hard struggle. It was much overdue, but had come at a price. No woman could be made a Bishop, any parish could prevent a woman ministering at their church by the parochial church council passing a formal resolution. The few priests who resigned in conscience over the issue were given overgenerous compensation. The legislation was drafted so badly that any priest who was prepared to sign that he was resigning over the issue could get the compensation. Some signed as a way of getting out, even though they were in favour of women priests.

My own brother was a leading layman in Forward in Faith which is the main organisation for those who are opposed to the ordination of women as priests. We still got on very well which proved the strength of our relationship and family ties.

We have a long way to go. Women will eventually be Bishops but we have only begun to realise that God cannot be male. We have lived so long in a patriarchal society that it will be a long time before we see what this means for the future. God is not female either of course. He or She is probably both, or more likely, neither is appropriate when talking of God.

There is even some truth in Dan Brown's the *The Da Vinci Code*. Most of course is nonsense. But there is truth in the charge that men in the Christian Church have deliberately downplayed the role of women in the early Church. Mary Magdalene was clearly far more important than most people have allowed, though the men who wrote the Gospels have not been able to deny that she and other women were the first witnesses of Christ's Resurrection. It is also true that male theologians down the centuries have not been sympathetic to the role of women. They have not been as bad as their Muslim counterparts, but the history of the Church has been written largely by men who had a very poor view of women. This has left its mark today, even with women now ordained as priests. So called Traditionalists are sometimes just misogynists, and are anyway relying on scripture as written and interpreted by men, which they fail to see has started the tradition they claim to be so sacred.

My wife Ann found the Church's attitude to women and gays particularly difficult and she became much more critical of the Church than I was. As an Archdeacon, though not hiding my beliefs, I had to be diplomatic, especially when meeting Evangelicals or Traditionalists.

Ann had a career change at this time. She gave up her job as a medical secretary and started to train as an Occupational Therapist at the London School of Occupational Therapy. She had never been to college, so she was able to get a very generous grant, which made it financially possible. After qualifying, she worked on Community Mental Health teams in Rotherhithe and Lewisham. She also began to garden seriously and transformed our garden at Dog Kennel Hill.

Long before the 1997 election I had got together a group of people to campaign for the Forgotten 30%. The group included the Bishops of Woolwich, Croydon and Willesden, as well as a number of London Archdeacons. We believed that whoever won the election was likely to be representing the 70% of the electorate who were relatively affluent and voted for policies which would help them, rather than the minority 30%. The latter were getting poorer and were largely forgotten by the electorate and politicians. The dangers of this needed to be brought to everyone's attention.

In the year before the election we each wrote a number of letters which were printed in *The Times*, *Guardian*, *Daily Telegraph*, *Independent* and other newspapers. Shortly before the election was announced, we held a conference at the Methodist Central Hall Westminster to brief Christians and to enable them to campaign for the Forgotten 30% during the Election. The *Independent* newspaper carried this report in March 1997:[19]

Senior officials of the Church of England yesterday accused politicians of all parties of divisive policies designed to appeal to the middle classes at the expense of those on the fringes of society, and pledged to put forward their own programme for dealing with poverty.

The Venerable Douglas Bartles-Smith, Archdeacon of Southwark, said, 'Members of Parliament must make clear how they plan to improve the lives of the "Forgotten 30%" – those people who are unemployed and economically inactive. All politicians talk of being tough on crime but they forget about the 30% of people, which is why there is crime in the first place.'

'The leaders of all three parties have recently said they are Christian and as Christians we are challenging them to put their faith into action.'

Newsnight covered the conference in a major way and the Bishop of Woolwich, Peter Hall, one of the conference speakers, spoke out strongly to a large audience.

The objective of the conference was to persuade those present to ask questions of candidates and to get the clergy to preach about the issue, highlighting it in any way they could. At the time I chaired the Editorial Board of the Diocesan Newspaper *The Bridge* which distributed 25,000 copies in South London and part of Surrey. So I wrote this editorial which went to every parish in the Diocese:

THE FORGOTTEN THIRTY PERCENT [20]

The political parties are now making their final preparations for a General Election which must be held soon.

So far, despite the moral stance of their recently declared Christian leaders, the politicians of all parties seem determined to appeal only to the 'self-interest' of the majority of the electorate. The well-being of the poorest in society – by best estimate some 30% of the population – is of secondary interest in the competitive scramble for the votes of the other 70%.

The Forgotten 30% are, to the government, an embarrassment whose very existence needs to be denied, while to the opposition, they are a liability whose cost dare not be mentioned. For they are in a minority – their votes do not count. The election will be decided by the more affluent 70%. It is scandalous that our leading politicians can, for this reason, ignore the needs of those who have little chance of finding adequately paid employment, of obtaining a decent home, of making their contribution to society and having their voice heard. Christians, however, cannot allow 30% of the population to be ignored. Any civilisation, any social and economic theory is judged by the Christian criterion of what it does, or does not do, for the poor. For as Reinhold Niebuhr said, 'who is better able to understand the true character of a civilisation than those who suffer most from its limitations?'

Politicians need to heed the warning of the recent Church of England report *Staying in the City* that the growing disparities of wealth and poverty will damage the economy and social fabric of the nation. We all need to be reminded that the prosperity most of us enjoy is due not simply to our own efforts but to the sacrifices of those who have gone before us, and ultimately to the Grace of God who remembered his people when they were homeless, landless, enslaved and oppressed. Christians therefore must use the run up to the General Election to educate our politicians – to remind them that we need a vision similar to the vision of the people of Israel as they entered the Promised Land, determined to build a just and fair society where the stranger was welcomed, where a real attempt was made to get rid of poverty and where everyone was provided with a family home which they could never lose. Above all we must seek out politicians of all political parties and demand from them their personal answer to the question 'What will you do about the Forgotten 30%?'

CHAPTER 9

❧✛❧

Change in the Diocese

EARLY in 1996 I received a letter from the Lord Chamberlain's office at Buckingham Palace inviting me to be a Chaplain to Her Majesty The Queen. I was delighted to accept, and was subsequently presented to Her Majesty at one of the Queen's garden parties in the summer. My wife Ann and son Peter were also presented and we met and talked to the Duke of Edinburgh and Prince Charles.

Queen's Chaplains wear scarlet cassocks which are paid for by the Queen. There is also a badge of office which is worn on the scarf. The College of Chaplains goes back to medieval times when the Monarch often used to travel round the country staying in the large country houses of the landed gentry. The Monarch would appoint a Royal Chaplain in each area where she stayed. Royal Chaplains have continued to be appointed since then from different parts of the country.

Today the Chaplains preach each year in either the Chapel Royal or the Queen's Chapel at St James Palace. On occasions we worship with the Queen and meet her afterwards at a reception for us and our spouses. We attend the Queen's Garden Party each year, robed in our scarlet cassocks. I continued to be a Chaplain and preach at the Chapel Royal after I retired as Archdeacon.

In 1997 some Christians, most of them Evangelicals, thought there would be a crisis in the Church of England if Prince Charles re-married. This was ridiculous, so I wrote the following letter which was published in *The Times* on August 9th:[1]

FROM THE ARCHDEACON OF SOUTHWARK

Sir, Church of England clergy who have divorced and remarried are allowed to continue their ministry in the Church. Why should there be a crisis in the Church of England if the Prince of Wales does the same?

The Diocese was to change considerably when the Bishops of Woolwich and Southwark announced their retirements in the middle of the decade. In 1996 Peter Hall retired and returned to Birmingham. We had worked well together largely because we shared the same beliefs on what was needed in the inner city. He was also a moderate Evangelical who listened to gay clergy and supported them. Indeed it was a very happy time for the whole of the Bishop's staff meeting. That is the Bishop and Archdeacons plus a few others who met regularly for the benefit of the whole Diocese. There was a good atmosphere and much helpful debate. David Gerrard was now Archdeacon of Wandsworth and we often worked together to see that important questions were raised and issues discussed. We sometimes disagreed, but mostly we were famous for working together and getting results. It was very different from Bishop Mervyn's day when Reg Bazire, one of his Archdeacons, told me he had nightmares and a sleepless night before every staff meeting.

Some hardline Evangelicals in the Diocese were opposed to the tolerant way in which gay clergy were supported, and they made their views clear to Bishop Roy and Archbishop George Carey. Roy Williamson did not let this affect the way he was dealing with the situation and they were anyway a small minority, but his days were numbered.

Bishop Roy decided to appoint a new Bishop of Woolwich before he retired. I was appointed a member of the committee to advise him. Bishop Roy wanted to appoint Colin Buchanan, and the Archbishop supported the appointment. Bishop Roy asked me what I thought. I perhaps surprised him by agreeing provided he did not upset the many clergy with gay partners in the Woolwich area. Bishop Roy said he had already made this clear to Colin, but he was very happy for me to see him before the appointment was announced. We met in a pub by the river near Southwark Cathedral. I made sure he knew what the situation was like in Southwark and said he should only come if he could accept this. He replied, 'I hear you, Douglas.'

I was sympathetic to Colin, who was a real Evangelical, because of what had happened to him when he was Bishop of Aston. Colin arranged for Archbishop Desmond Tutu to lead a Mission to Birmingham. This was a very imaginative and enterprising thing to do. At the time however, the right wing press were critical of Desmond Tutu, and racism in Birmingham meant it was opposed by some white people. The Mission was still supported by many thousands of Christians, but it made a financial loss because of the opposition of some. Bishop Colin therefore resigned and his resignation was surprisingly accepted by the Bishop of Birmingham. Many of us in Southwark were critical of the Bishop of Birmingham's decision and sympathised with Colin, who we felt had been badly treated. We invited Colin to attend our three day staff meeting where we made clear our support. Colin then went to be a Vicar in Kent.

On the whole Colin kept his word when he became the Bishop of Woolwich. He could not of course hide his own belief that gay clergy should be celibate, and he withstood all my efforts, in our regular Bible studies together, to show him what in my view the Bible was really saying. We disagreed strongly and I did not mince my words. But Colin has a gift for getting on with people he disagrees with, and it is impossible to dislike him even when you think his opinions quite wrong.

The retirement of Bishop Roy Williamson in 1997 gave the Archbishop of Canterbury George Carey his chance to intervene in Southwark Diocese. It was the time of the lead up to the 1998 Lambeth Conference, when in an atmosphere described by the Bishop of Worcester as like a Nuremberg rally, the Bishops of the Anglican Communion sided with homophobia. Many of them will deny this of course, but for me and many others, telling gay priests they cannot have sex with their partners is homophobia and a denial of their human rights. Just as discriminating against black people is racism, so discriminating against gay and lesbian people is homophobia.

In Southwark therefore we were understandably nervous about what the Crown Appointments Commission would do. They meet in secret together with four representatives of the Diocese. They study papers which have been prepared by the Prime Minster's and Archbishop's appointments secretaries, who consult widely in the Diocese beforehand.

It was clear that the majority of people in Southwark wished the radical tradition of the Diocese to be continued. Dr Rowan Williams who was then Bishop of Monmouth was the person most people wanted. Indeed he was one of the two names sent to Tony Blair at 10 Downing Street. The other was Tom Butler the Bishop of Leicester. But it is said that neither candidate had a clear majority. This gave the Archbishop of Canterbury his chance to bring Southwark into line with the policy of the House of Bishops on homosexuality. The views of Rowan Williams were different and in the public domain. In 1989 he gave the Michael Harding Memorial address as Lady Margaret Professor of Divinity at Oxford when he said:[2]

Anyone who knows the complexities of the true celibate vocation would be the last to have any sympathy with the extraordinary idea that sexual orientation is an automatic pointer to the celibate life; almost as if celibacy before God is less costly, even less risky, for the homosexual than the heterosexual ... if we are looking for a sexual ethic that can seriously be informed by our Bible, there is a good deal to steer us away from assuming that reproductive sex is a norm, however important and theologically significant it may be . . . if we are afraid of facing the reality of same-sex love because it compels us to think through the processes of bodily desire and delight in their own right, perhaps we ought to be more cautious about appealing to scripture as legitimating only pro-creative heterosexuality.

In a church which accepts the legitimacy of contraception, the absolute condemnation of same-sex relations of intimacy must rely either on abstract fundamentalist deployment of a number of very ambiguous texts or on a problematic and non-scriptural theory about natural complementarity, applied narrowly and crudely to physical differentiation without regard to psychological structures.

Rowan when he became Bishop of Monomouth never repudiated this talk, and Bishop Tom was eventually asked to be the Bishop of Southwark. His initial view of the Diocese was that it seemed to be deeply divided between liberals and Conservative Evangelicals. But one wonders what he was told. For he gave the impression it needed cleaning out like the Augean stables. The result was that Tom came in with the very hard line that gay priests would only be appointed if they were celibate.

The Conservative Evangelicals were over the moon with delight, but at his first staff meeting all the Archdeacons strongly opposed the hard line taken by Bishop Tom. It was a very uncomfortable three days at Wych-croft. Bishop Colin not unnaturally felt he could now openly support Bishop Tom, so the Bishops were ranged against the Archdeacons. David Gerrard and I worked very closely together at this critical time, and we tried to give the gay and lesbian clergy as much support as we could.

However during his first six months Bishop Tom went round the Diocese and began to see for himself what it was like. People made their positions clear and asked him many questions. He realised he needed to be careful and was sensible enough not to go in for a witch hunt. He was nevertheless determined not to appoint any more gay clergy with partners as incumbents. For Tom's first two years therefore the Archdeacons supported the gay clergy, and some kept from the Bishops information which they considered it unwise to pass on.

In the light of the position of the Archbishop and the Bishops I had no qualms about advising gay clergy to lie if necessary. This is what 'Situation Ethics' demands when the Church takes up such a ridiculous position.

Bishop Tom however gradually began to change as he really got to know the people of the Diocese. A clear majority of priests and lay people opposed the Archbishop and Bishop's line, and he had to accommodate himself to this a little. He still held the line, but he also became much more supportive of gay clergy.

By the time of my retirement, Bishop Tom was viewed much more kindly by gay clergy in the Diocese, and it was Archbishop Rowan Williams who was criticised. This was because of the appointment of Dr Jeffrey John to be Bishop of Reading. Bishop Tom had given his support to this appointment. He knew that although Jeffrey had a partner, they were now celibate, and Jeffrey was prepared to follow the guidelines the Bishops had insisted upon. Jeffrey had in fact been celibate for a number of years, which caused me to tease him by suggesting he was letting the side down. He was a member of the Bishop's staff meeting, was respected by many of Southwark's Evangelicals, and often quite conservative.

However, all this was not good enough for fundamentalist Evangelicals in the rest of the country who created a great rumpus, as did Conservative Evangelicals in Africa, the Global South and the West Indies. Many of us urged Jeffrey not to withdraw. The appointment had been made by the Queen and the Archbishop could not prevent the appointment unless Jeffrey resigned. But Jeffrey was ambushed by Rowan Williams at Lambeth Palace and his withdrawal was forced. Jeffrey asked to speak to Bishop Tom. Bishop Tom tried to get through to Lambeth Palace to prevent Jeffrey's reisgnation. He was eventually allowed to speak on the phone. But in the end Jeffrey gave in.

People in Southwark were furious with Rowan, but greatly apprecia-tive of what Bishop Tom had done. From now on he had much more support from the people of the Diocese. We all did what we could for Jeffrey and his partner, who needed support in a situation which was not of their making and had been badly managed. In recent years I have often felt ashamed of the Church of England, but this was dreadful.

I was very annoyed also with Colin Buchanan who, almost alone in the leadership of the Diocese, backed those who said the appointment should not have been made. Apparently, according to Colin, being celibate was not enough, you actually had to agree with the line taken by the Bishop's mafia. Jeffrey could not be a Bishop because of what he had said in the past, and because this was well known.

But the Conservative Evangelicals of course were not finished. They were soon protesting at the consecration of the first openly gay Bishop in the United States. The Anglican Church in America was not in the business of discriminating against gay people, and therefore agreed to consecrate Gene Robinson, who had a partner, as Bishop of New Hampshire. The Canadian Anglican Church also decided that it would allow all its Dioceses to follow New Hampshire's lead and authorise the blessing of same sex partnerships. Evangelical fundamentalists in Africa and the Global South threatened schism. But instead of making a stand, Rowan Williams caved in to try to keep the Anglican Communion together. This was a major mistake as I shall argue in the final chapter.

I had worked with Tom Butler before when he was the national Bishop responsible for *Faith in the City* and its follow up. We had an uneasy relationship at first, as already explained, but later we got on well especially on matters to do with social responsibility. I was chair of the Diocesan Board for Church in Society, and we worked together to regenerate the inner city. Bishop Tom also wanted to see more black people holding positions of responsibility in the Diocese.

Following the murder of Stephen Lawrence, the Macpherson Report suggested it was not just the police force that was institutionally racist. So Bishop Tom urged the Diocesan Synod to set up an independent inquiry into institutional racism within the structures of the Diocese of Southwark. The resulting report made specific recommendations which aimed to increase black representation on electoral rolls, on PCC's and Deanery Synods, and to increase the number of black clergy. It also recommended training in racial awareness for key Diocesan staff. The report was chaired by Sir Herman Ousley, the chairman of the Commission for Racial Equality and an Anglican who lived in Southwark Archdeaconry. Delbert Sandiford was then appointed to manage the implementation of the report's recommendations. He worked closely with the Black and Minority Ethnic Forum which had been set up much earlier. This was increasingly important as many inner city Anglican churches were now black majority churches.

Very soon the numbers of black people seeking ordination increased quite substantially, as did the number of black members of Parochial Church Councils and Churchwardens. The Bishop's staff meeting also became more representative. Archdeacon Danny Kajumba joined Bishop Wilfred Wood as a second black person and Christine Hardman was appointed the first woman Archdeacon. She joined Wendy Robins the Director of Communications and Resources and Linda Borthwick the Director of Education who had been members for a few years.

Bishop Tom also gave strong support to the campaign to keep the Octavia Hill estate flats and houses affordable to poor people. As we have seen already these were owned by the Church Commissioners. The Walworth estate was a shining example of the Church's commitment to housing 100 years ago, which still today has much to teach those who designed and managed the 1960s housing which surrounds it.

In 1903 a 100 year old lease expired on 22 acres of estate owned by the Church Commissioners and described then by *The Times* newspaper as 'one of the most crowded of those South London slums which have engaged the attention and taxed the studied moderation of Mr Charles Booth.'

The potential for redevelopment of the area, so totally different from what it was at the beginning of the 19th century, was enormous. Nevertheless the Church Commissioners were persuaded by Octavia Hill not to sell the freehold to developers but to redevelop the area themselves, widening and re-arranging the streets, including a co-op shop, setting aside an area for recreation, an area for a new school, and accommodation for 790 families in four roomed and three roomed cottages, and in cottage flats and three storey tenement houses. Octavia was invited to manage the properties to add to the Church Commissioners housing she already managed, including the large Waterloo estate which she took over at four days notice in 1901.

The Church Commissioners said at the time that 'they recognised that the possession of very large areas of land, some of it situated in districts convenient for the houses of the poorer classes, imposes on them the moral obligation of seeing that the claims of the working classes to be provided with healthy homes, in places convenient for their occupation and at reasonable rents, should be respected.'

Even then the Commissioners did not come to this conclusion without pressure being applied. In 1904 *The Times* newspaper reported:

The management of Church estates has recently come in for its share of denunciation. The falling in of some leases of old houses, behind the abbey led to a rising of the antiquaries and to a reply from the Church Commissioners 'that it was bound to dispose of property to the best advantages'. The state of the property in Walworth has brought no little odium upon the Church though in actual fact nothing could be done by the Commissioners to improve it till the lease was out. Nothing however could have been more fatal to the prestige of the Church than that the present opportunity of illustrating the responsibilities of property, especially when it is vested in Christian people, should be omitted in favour of what would 'pay' best. Besides the Commission is after all a public body, under parliamentary supervision, and it cannot divest itself of the duty of considering the needs of the people as well as the extension of the Church, nor could anything be worse than that the Church should be extended in one diocese at the cost of demoralisation of people in another.

We argued with the Church Commissioners that this was as true today as one hundred years ago, when they, like their predecessors, tried to claim their obligations to do whatever will 'pay' best in order to pay the clergy. We said they had a moral obligation to keep the rents affordable to poor people.

We started gently when I asked Simon Hughes to ask a question of the Commissioners in the House of Commons. This he did. Simon is an excellent Member of Parliament who, as member for Southwark and Bermondsey, has often worked with me. He was also an Anglican. Next, some of us walked through the estates from St Peter Walworth to St John's Waterloo where a service was held to remember Octavia Hill, and I preached a strong sermon asking the Church Commissioners to honour Octavia's legacy.

I had appointed the Reverend Benny Hazlehurst as an Archdeaconry Estate Worker to assist parishes to work better with those who lived on the many estates in the Borough of Southwark. He spoke at both the Board for Church in Society and the Diocesan Synod, persuading them to vote overwhelmingly to ask the Church Commissioners to change their minds. He worked with the tenant's leaders to organise three demonstrations outside Lambeth Palace and outside the Church Commissioners. The latter was preceded by a march, and was followed by a meeting at the Church Commissioners. Simon Hughes and some Borough Councillors were also present.

Meanwhile Bishop Tom and I met with the Church Commissioners. Tom was very angry, blunt and outspoken in his criticism. I spoke equally strongly stressing the moral obligation the Commissioners had. In the end the matter went to the Archbishop's Council, but only a few small concessions were made. However Bishop Tom had been seen to side with local inner city people, and this stood him in good stead with the people in the Diocese.

This was not the only occasion when Simon Hughes worked closely with me and other Christians in Southwark. He had represented Southwark and Bermondsey ever since he beat Peter Tatchell. The Labour party lost the seat as some prominent old Labour party members campaigned against their own candidate because he was gay. I was pleased they were never able to get the seat back from Simon.

This was mainly because Simon worked so hard. I have never known another Member of Parliament who knew the people of his area so well. He was therefore deservedly popular. He was also brave, speaking out against criminal gangs and urging witnesses to come forward. For a time he had police protection because of this stand. I never went to an event in his constituency when he was not present. In other constituencies with other Members of Parliament this was far from being the case. I greatly enjoyed preaching at the service in Southwark Cathedral to celebrate his twenty one years as a Member of Parliament.

Nowhere was my relationship with Bishop Tom more important than when I chaired the Editorial Advisory Board of the Diocesan Newspaper. I had been chair of Communications and Resources for some years, but it was when we appointed Wendy Robins as Director that the possibility of having a Diocesan Newspaper arose. Bishop Roy Williamson was very much in favour, but the Communications and Resources committee took some time researching what was happening in other Dioceses. Three models were finally looked at very carefully, and eventually a contract was signed with the Kent Christian Press. They were not only the best value for money, but also left the control of the newspaper and what went into it completely in our hands.

Wendy Robins was appointed Managing Editor and Bryan Harris, who ran Kent Christian Press, was the Editor. There was also an Editorial Advisory Board which I chaired. The members of the Board were chosen by the Communications and Resources committee. Every edition would be read by myself and Wendy Robins before it went to print. The Bishop would hold us responsible for getting this right. It proved to be quite a difficult task on occasions, though we were helped by the guidelines agreed by the Editorial Advisory Board.

We were determined to have a lively newspaper in which people would be able to express their own views, especially in the letters pages, and we would not dodge difficult issues like homosexuality. Nevertheless we would not print sexist, racist, or homophobic comment, nor of course would we print libel. A decision not to print, or more likely amend material had to be taken very quickly by Wendy and me. This led to some lively conversations on the telephone when decisions had to be made.

We had an excellent Editorial Advisory Board which included a good representation from across the Diocese; women like Betty Percival and Denise Mumford who had been Director of Welcare; black people like

Canon Ivor Smith-Cameron, Canon Francis Makambwe and Jeremy Blunden; liberal catholics such as the journalist Tom Sutcliffe and Bishop Hugh Montefiore; Evangelicals such as Christopher Skilton and Paul Perkin.

The board planned each edition of the paper when 25,000 copies were printed every month and distributed to the parishes. The paper was called *The Bridge* because the Editorial Board wanted to bridge the divide between the centre of the Diocese and the parishes. First it wanted the Bishops, the Diocesan Synod and the Boards of the Diocese to explain their decisions to the parishes, and then we wanted the people of the parish to express their views whenever possible. Difficult decisions of policy were taken by the Board, or if Wendy and I had to do so, which happened occasionally, our decision would be discussed at the next Board meeting and either backed or not.

There was a lot of debate on the Board about the features we should do. Hugh Montefiore, Ivor Smith-Cameron, Tom Sutcliffe and Denise Mumford in particular had all kinds of exciting ideas. Some were sensible, some not, but in the end we usually produced a very good newspaper which was certainly better than that produced by any other Diocese. I used to read some of the others and they were mainly about selling the Diocesan line rather than encouraging the radical debate which we were used to in Southwark.

Each month a member of the Editorial Board was chosen to write the editorial on a subject we all agreed, and usually was on the feature chosen for the central spread of the newspaper. My editorial on the Forgotten 30% has already been featured. Two others will follow in this chapter.

The Communications and Resources committee also tackled stewardship and in particular assisted parishes with raising the money they required to pay the clergy and cover their own costs. A DIY course called TRIO was particularly effective. The department had invented it and it sold well in other dioceses. We also arranged meetings around the Diocese to encourage the parishes to do better. I wrote this editorial in the Bridge before we set out on a round of six meetings in different parts of the Diocese:

No Crisis[3]

The parishes of the Diocese are to be congratulated on paying 99.9% of their parish share in the Fairer Shares scheme in 2002 and possibly doing even better in 2003. There is therefore no financial crisis in the Diocese. In 2001 a series of 'Facing the Future' meetings were held to look at the financial situation in order to agree how we should respond to the decrease in monies which were coming to us from the national church. That consultation process resulted in cuts of £1,000,000 in spending and the parishes agreeing to provide an extra £500,000 income to the Diocese.

It is encouraging that parishes are proving they can pay the extra which was agreed – nevertheless, the Communications and Resources department are holding six meetings this month (see centre pages) because we believe that our incumbents, churchwardens, treasurers and stewardship secretaries have a vital role to play in ensuring that each parish has sufficient financial resources to meet the challenges of the future and fulfil God's mission in their locality. Through these meetings, and the centre pages of this edition, we hope to provide you all with encouragement to take back to your parishes on the financial situation in the Diocese.

We want to give you information about the future of the national church and how it will affect our Diocese. We want to provide you with the necessary materials to help you to share this with the members of your parish, in order to encourage them to review their giving, and see how their giving to the church helps to further God's mission in Southwark Diocese.

But most important of all we want to hear from you about your views on the financing of the parochial ministry and how those at Diocesan level can best help you to work at financing God's mission in the coming years.

The six meetings were well attended. Two were chaired by Bishop Tom and four by myself. People were particularly helped by the materials provided by Communications and Resources. The chair of the Board of Finance Andrew Britton and Wendy Robbins spoke only after we had rehearsed the presentation very thoroughly so that it went well. This was important, but the most important people in making sure each parish paid its fair share were the Archdeacons.

First we needed to ensure that the system was fully explained to each parish when every three years their parish share was worked out. Each Archdeacon chaired a meeting at which John Henson, who was in charge, explained the system. It was based on two facts. How many people attended the church each month and how much those people earned. To find this out the Archdeacons asked the churchwardens each year to do a congregational count on eight successive Sundays. Each parish also asked its congregation to fill in a simple and anonymous form which revealed how much they earned.

This was followed by a meeting of parish representatives with two trained lay people from another parish representing the Diocese. The Archdeacon was usually present to see fair play. The meeting agreed a membership number and a financial category for the parish. These were of course based on the forms which had previously been filled in.

When I became Archdeacon a number of parishes were in debt to the diocese for failing to pay their parish share. It is the Archdeacon's job to see that the debt is paid. Within two years of my arrival every parish in the Archdeaconry was paying on time and this remained true for the next fifteen years whilst I was Archdeacon.

I also prepared statistics each year based on the congregational counts which were sent to me. As it was done partly for financial reasons, no parish exaggerated their figures. But even so the numbers attending church in the Archdeaconry went up more or less every year. I stress this because Liberal Catholics like myself are sometimes accused of not bothering about whether the Church grows. I did bother very much, and as we have already seen, the number of people attending church increased when I was a vicar in Camberwell and Battersea, and in the Archdeaconry when I was Archdeacon of Southwark. I might add that there were a few Evangelical parishes in the Archdeaconry, but most were Catholic.

I had an interest in statistics and for many years was a member of the Council of Reference for *Religious Trends* which was published by Christian Research and edited by Peter Brierley. Providing these statistics was one way of countering the secular media which usually down played the strength of the churches in our society.

When I was Vicar of St Lukes Battersea I tried to tackle this in a light-hearted way when I wrote the following letter to *The Times* which was broadcast on radio and picked up by other newspapers:

The Wages of Virtue[4]
FROM THE REV. D. L. BARTLES-SMITH

Sir, Match of the Day is watched by only 6,250,000 people. *Songs of Praise* is watched by ten million. Football has been offered £5,300,000 by the television companies. Does this not mean the churches should be offered £7 million?

The Government Census in 2001 did make some people see the strength of Christianity when 72% of people described themselves as Christian. Even the *Guardian* newspaper observed, 'This is a Christian country simply in the unanswerable sense that most of its citizens think of themselves as Christians.' This argues for the Establishment of the Church to continue as 26 million of these people will have been baptised as Anglicans.

This may help to explain why Rowan Williams' appointment as Archbishop of Canterbury was greeted with so much enthusiasm. People may not go to church but an intelligent Archbishop could still

speak to 72% of people who said they were Christian. In a *Bridge* editorial
I argued that Rowan could do this:

Christians Face Intellectual Crisis[5]

'If there's one thing I long for above all else', said Dr Rowan Williams when
nominated as Archbishop of Canterbury, 'It's that the years to come may see
Christianity in this country able again to capture the imagination of our
culture.'

The need for this is very clear from a study of the statistics supplied by
Christian Research. The Decade of Evangelism has clearly failed to halt the
decline in church attendance. London, it is true, is doing better than the rest of
the country but there is no sign yet of the decline coming to an end.

Nevertheless, we can be encouraged by some recent statistics published by
Christian Research in *Religion Trends 3*. Belief in God remains remarkably
robust (67% of the population), 35% of babies are baptised; 54% of first mar-
riages take place in church; 75% of funerals are held with a Christian ceremony
and 60% of people still consider themselves to be Christian even though most
don't attend church regularly. These statistics are a sign that there is a spiritual
hunger in the community which can be met if tackled in the right way.

Bishop Paul Richardson writing recently in the Church of England
Newspaper, gives us a clue about the way forward. 'Christianity in Britain', he
says, 'faces an intellectual crisis of credibility. Evangelical churches are well
attended but while evangelicals can build up successful parishes of committed,
like minded people, they are less able to convince the population at large of the
truth or value of Christianity.

This is why Dr Rowan Williams' appointment is so important. He is a
theologian of the first rank with the ability to communicate to intelligent
people outside the church. He is well able to encourage attempts to re-
interpret the Christian faith in contemporary terms and to experiment with
new forms of mission. He is likely to adopt a position of critical solidarity
towards government policies while seeking to influence public opinion so that
a more radical approach to serious social problems may become possible.

All this can best be achieved through retaining the Established church
especially now that we have seen 72% of the population claim to be
Christian. Many including the Archbishop are not sure about this, but in
an article in the South London Press I argued as follows:

Established Church is there to help us all[6]

The Established Church is a public symbol of the importance of religion, of
belief in God and of the limits of the State's sovereignty. It is important because
it challenges the dominant secular materialism of our time. This is why many
Hindus, Muslin, Sikhs and Jews as well as Christians from other denomin-

ations, would prefer the Establishment to remain. But the Established Church is not just about Bishops in the House of Lords, or the Queen being the supreme governor of the Church of England. It is also about the rights of ordinary people.

If you live in England you have a right, if you wish, to have your funeral in your local parish church. You don't have to accept a rushed service at the local crematorium where only a small amount of time is allowed for each funeral. There can be a well prepared service of reasonable length conducted by the local Vicar in the church where you live, followed afterwards by a short committal at either the crematorium or the graveside.

Everyone also has the right to have their child christened in their parish church. This is a legal right we all have, and no Vicar is allowed to refuse to baptise any child who lives in the parish. If he or she did, then you can complain to the Bishop or Archdeacon who must then see the baptism carried out.

If you are christened you have a further right to be married in the parish church where either you or your partner lives. Every South Londoner has these rights because the Church of England is Established. This means that each Vicar is entrusted with the 'Care of souls' of everyone who lives within the parish boundaries.

A Church of England church therefore, more than any other, exists for the benefit of those who do not go to church as well as those who do.

So the next time you hear of people who want to get rid of the Established Church, it might be worth reminding them of the rights they will be losing. For, by law, the Church of England is there for everyone.

❧✝❧

CHAPTER 10

The Archdeacon's Role

ARCHDEACONS are most well known for the part they play in Ecclesiastical law and especially faculties. Many people don't know that Ecclesiastical law is part of the law of the land or that it can apply in some unexpected places.

Lambeth Council discovered this when they thought they could do what they liked in South Norwood Cemetery. The Archdeacon of Lambeth Richard Bird discovered some workmen destroying some monuments and gravestones which could only be touched if a faculty had been obtained from the Chancellor of the Diocese. The Archdeacon ordered them to stop work. They did not do so. The Archdeacon reported what had happened to the Chancellor of the Diocese who made them stop, and ordered Lambeth Council to appear before him at an Ecclesiastical court which he held at the Old Bailey.

Many people also don't realise that if human remains are buried in consecrated ground in any cemetery, then they can only be moved when the Chancellor's permission has been obtained. It is becoming quite common for people to ask for their families' human remains to be moved when they move house. This is being rightly resisted, and Chancellors will only agree in exceptional circumstances.

The Chancellor of the Diocese is an Ecclesiastical Court Judge. He or she has to be at least a QC and quite often is a Judge in a secular court. He is assisted by the Registrar and Legal Officer of the Diocese and the Archdeacons.

If any changes to a church or building on church land are proposed, a faculty (ecclesiastical planning permission) is required. The Archdeacon is informed, and the matter goes to the Diocesan Advisory Committee for the Care of Churches, before an application for faculty is sent to the Chancellor, or the Archdeacon in minor cases, for a decision. Before that decision however, a citation has to be put up outside the church so that anyone who wishes to object to the Chancellor can do so.

This is a very important safeguard which ensures that a Vicar and parochial church council cannot ride roughshod over other parishioners without their voice being heard; if there are objections, the Chancellor can hear them in an Ecclesiastical court and then decide what should be done.

The Diocesan Advisory Committee for the Care of Churches is composed of representatives of English Heritage, the Victorian, Georgian and other Conservation societies, the Diocesan Synod, the local Council, as well as church architects, others with professional expertise and the Archdeacons. The latter are particularly important in representing the pastoral dimension.

But it is also part of the Archdeacon's job to see that the whole system works. In recent years in Southwark Diocese we have found it helpful to call a site meeting of everyone involved before the process starts. This is especially necessary when major works are being undertaken. In this way the views of the Heritage bodies are known from the beginning. Sometimes this means that a project is not pursued because there is so much criticism, and it is clear the project would not be approved. More likely it might be modified, or a parish might proceed knowing that objections were likely, and therefore a Consistory Court (Ecclesiastical Court) possible. If the latter, at least a parish was forewarned and opposition would not be a surprise.

Borough Councils need to know about the system. Councils have turned some graveyards into small parks and manage them, but don't always know that changes must be approved through a faculty. This was important not least because the land in some areas was ripe for re-development, and we were then able to ensure parks were preserved for the benefit of the local community.

There were also three church buildings in Southwark Archdeaconry which were not owned by the Church of England, but they were all subject to faculty jurisdiction. Without this, the owners could have done what they liked with the churches concerned, and in at least one case would have done so. I stress this for many are critical of the system. Evangelicals in particular want to alter churches sometimes without giving any weight to the views of those who wish to preserve our heritage. Happy clappy services are an abomination to many, but even happy clappies should see that there are limits to what should be done inside a Grade I listed building. The Church of England is privileged to look after its historic churches for the nation, but we must not abuse this privilege.

One final point: the Chancellor takes the decision in the end, not the

Diocesan Advisory Committee. Sometimes the Archdeacon needs to remind both a parish and the Advisory Committee of this. A parish may ask the Chancellor for a faculty even if the Diocesan Advisory Committee is against it. There was an occasion when I disagreed so strongly with a recommendation of the Diocesan Advisory Committee, that I told them I would write to the Chancellor asking him to disregard their decision.

This was because Christ's Chapel Dulwich, next door to the famous Dulwich Picture Gallery, wished to assist with the necessary alterations to the Gallery. But the Advisory Committee felt these were detrimental to Christ's Chapel. All the necessary permissions except faculty had been obtained, and the gallery was about to lose its finance for the project when the Chancellor agreed with me and granted the faculty.

Ecclesiastical law also governs three different kinds of church property. The church buildings themselves are subject to various measures which are administered by the Church Commissioners. Vicarages are looked after by the Diocese, but an incumbent has certain rights both in regard to the vicarage and the church, provided he or she has been inducted into the freehold of the living. Church halls and other property are either Diocesan Glebe, or more likely held by a Diocesan Trust on behalf of a parish. No parish is allowed to own land directly. All this can be a legal minefield, and any parish which employs a solicitor who does not know Ecclesiastical law is very foolish. The Archdeacon is there to guide any parish through this minefield.

In Southwark I was for many years Chair of the Sites and Redundant Churches Uses Committee. Its job was to advise parishes on property matters and to take decisions on redundant church buildings. It was the only committee which dealt with the whole site with all three types of church property present. It met every two months and included the Diocesan Registrar, Secretary and Surveyor, other surveyors and property experts and all the Archdeacons.

It was very important in preventing major disasters. Parishes can quite easily get themselves into bad debt when trying to manage a large building project like a new church. So we looked very carefully at every new building. Many new churches were being built, and always cost more than the parish anticipated. We insisted that parishes had the money to pay for a project before it started. We then monitored progress carefully. Major redevelopment of existing listed buildings could be even more costly, especially when destroyed by fire.

I remember arriving at St Barnabas Church Dulwich to see the roof go up in flames. I stood with horrified parishioners before the Vicar was able to arrive. They were of course stunned, and perhaps it was just as well that they were unable to see the future at that moment. For although everyone wants to rebuild as soon as possible when this happens, the procedures which have to be gone through are very daunting.

English Heritage wanted the tower to remain. After much discussion and debate the Chancellor eventually agreed it could be demolished like the rest of the building which still stood. The local council was difficult about planning permission for the new church. Some people disliked the design including members of the Diocesan Advisory Committee. The Archdeacon's role is often crucial at such times in getting things decided and done. I had meetings with the Chief Executive of the council, the Chancellor, the Vicar and Churchwardens to move matters on. Eventually a magnificent new church with a unique glass spire was the result.

The Sites Committee also dealt with redundant churches. Before my time the old St George's Church in Camberwell had been sold for a pittance to a Black Led Church. This was done for the best of reasons, but it was a ridiculous thing to do. For as the Church of England had been unable to repair a Grade I listed building, how could a church with less resources do so?

The Pentecostal Church eventually ceased to worship there, and the building began to fall down. Children would break into the crypt and rifle the old coffins and drag them outside. On one occasion a baby's coffin was discovered outside the church with the baby well preserved and looking as if he had only just died. Some of the people buried in the church had died of smallpox and therefore this was a health hazard.

An outcry followed, and everyone agreed that the Black Led Church should either look after the building properly or sell it to people who could. However the Black Led Church wanted to sell at market value even though they had been given the church for a pittance. It took many years of careful negotiations, involving both English Heritage and the Church Commissioners, before the matter could be sorted and the church sold to a housing association. They converted it into flats, keeping the outside of the building exactly as it had always been.

In my time as chair therefore, we insisted on a proper market value for all the redundant churches which were sold. Many still went to Black Led Churches who because they paid the market price were sub-sequently able to look after the building. There was sometimes still a problem from vandalism whilst we tried to sell a church. At St Bartholomew's Bermondsey young people continually broke into the building to use it as a playground. We had to spend a lot of money to hire a guard to protect the building while we tried to sell it.

In dealing with churches that are no longer needed it was always necessary to consult with the local community. There was nearly always some protest if a church had to be pulled down, even when another church was going to be built. The protest usually came from those who did not go to church regularly rather than those who did. We can never overestimate what church buildings mean to people locally – especially those who do not often attend them. People who go to church, go not only for themselves, but for those also who are just glad the church is there.

One of the most vital jobs of an Archdeacon is to see that child protection procedures are being observed. He or she must check that every parish has a Child Protection Officer and a plan which follows national guidelines and which has been approved by the Parochial Church Council.

Questions about child protection were asked in the Articles of Enquiry which the Archdeacon sends Churchwardens to fill in: Were two adults always present when children's activities took place? Did other organisations who used the building have their own child protection policies? Had the Child Protection Officer been to one of the training conferences arranged by the Diocese?

Some parishes found it difficult to find two adults to be present, but the Archdeacon had to insist that this was done or the activity closed down. Later when the government brought in its own legislation insisting on checks, Archdeacons had to make sure that parishes were complying. The Diocese ran checks on all its clergy, but the parishes had to see that checks were carried out on all lay people in contact with young people.

This was a huge task and at first some parishes were not good at doing it. They had to be warned that if this was not done, the Ecclesiastical Insurance Company would not cover them for negligence. It took time, but in the end all the parishes I was responsible for were cooperating fully.

Archdeacons are very much involved in the appointment of new Incumbents. I always met the Parochial Church Council soon after their Vicar announced his or her retirement. I did this to make sure they fully understood the method of appointment in the Church of England which is quite complicated. The laity in particular sometimes don't know of the rights they have in the process. I would give every Parochial Church Councillor a short booklet which explained the procedures but underline the crucial points myself.

The Parochial Church Council needed to produce an attractive booklet about the parish which included the job description and person specification for the incumbent they wanted. They also needed to take great care over electing the two people who would act as their representatives. For once elected these two lay people met with the candidates and decided whether to accept or reject the person whom the Patron of the Benefice nominated. I explained that this could be done in two ways. The Patron might see candidates and then send one to the representatives of the parish to interview, or the Patron might interview the candidates with the parish representatives. In either case it was the Patron who nominated a candidate and the parish representatives who said yes or no.

Later I met with the parish representatives, when elected, to give them advice on the best way to interview candidates. I suggested they took the candidates on a tour of the parish showing them and their spouses the vicarage and the church. That should be followed by lunch when candidates could meet other staff and churchwardens if they were not representatives. Formal interviews could follow in the afternoon.

Patrons, when they were not the Bishop, sometimes needed guidance on the procedures. We would always arrange a meeting with the Parochial Church Council and the Patron with the Bishop, Archdeacon and Rural Dean also present, so that we could all discuss the situation before the job was advertised.

Representatives were sometimes not quite sure whether to accept or reject a candidate. I always told them they could talk to me confidentially if this was the case. I would not influence them at all but would help them to make up their own minds. Sometimes I suggested they had another meeting with the candidate to ask further questions.

Priests who did not get the job need to know the reasons. It was often the case that they were very good priests but their skills did not match what a particular parish was looking for. I can remember interviewing people when we all agreed a particular person was the most gifted, yet we also agreed he was not the right person for a particular job. Clergy need to be told this or they begin to feel rejected, which is often not the case at all.

In Southwark the Archdeacons were also very much involved in annual interviews with the clergy who were seen in a four year cycle, twice by the Archdeacon, once by the Bishop and once by a trained lay person. The format of the interview changed a little over the years, but it always involved looking back at targets set the preceding year, and subsequently setting targets for the coming year. Clergy were sent an assessment form before the interview, but it was filled in an signed during the interview itself.

These were not quite assessment interviews as done in the secular world for at least two reasons. A person doing an assessment interview in the business world would normally do no more than ten a year. We did forty-fifty interviews a year. Similarly in the secular world the achievement of targets would be related to pay. Again this was not the case in the Church. Nevertheless the interviews were helpful in ensuring clergy were seen on a regular basis and encouraged in their work.

Interviews only started in the late 1980s and at first clergy were very sceptical. I remember the Provost of Southwark David Edwards saying to me, 'Do you really think people will come; won't you have to drop in on them for a cup of tea?' In fact they came and found the hour long interview helpful, especially with the Archdeacons. We know this, because the system was reviewed two years before I retired, and the Archdeacons were seen by the clergy as the best at the task.

In the Southwark Archdeaconry I also carried out two-day Visitations of each parish. I did six a year and the Bishop two, and they happened every 5 years. This meant I visited every parish in the Archdeaconry formally during my time as Archdeacon. It was probably the most important task we did.

The visit started when I celebrated the Eucharist and preached on the Sunday morning and met the congregation. It finished with a meeting of the Parochial Church Council on the Monday night when three targets for the next five years were set. Before the visit the Parochial Church Council filled in a long questionnaire which I discussed with them before they set their own targets.

I would conduct this exercise myself to ensure we heard the true voice of the laity. After prayer, I would ask every Parochial Church Councillor to write down on a piece of paper the two targets they felt the church needed to have. These were then collected by one person who read them all out. What was said was put up on a flip chart. Quite often it was clear immediately what the three targets should be. Always it started a debate which led quite quickly to agreement on the three targets. The priests were allowed to participate, but not to dominate the discussions.

For the rest of the time I had meetings with Churchwardens and other leaders, often over a meal. I toured the parish on the Monday and met with people in schools, community centres, tenant associations and other churches. The Vicar always came with me, and it soon became clear how well she knew her parish and how well people knew her.

After the visit I wrote a letter which was read out at the next Parochial Church Council meeting. It outlined my impressions and reminded them to discuss their targets further at coming meetings so they could decide how they were going to implement them.

Most of the parishes were Catholic, but a few were Evangelical, and you might wonder how I got on. The answer is surprisingly well, perhaps because I was very careful to be even-handed. Bishop Colin believed I was too helpful to some of the Evangelical parishes, and that may well have been the case as I was determined my churchmanship should not be an issue.

One of the leaders of the Conservative Evangelical group Reform was in the Archdeaconry, and we had a good relationship. I preached a very biblical sermon when I went to his church. He knew my views, and I knew his, but neither of us made a meal of it. Similarly two parishes in the Archdeaconry were opposed to the ordination of women priests, and had voted to come under the Extended Episcopal Care of the Bishop of Fulham, who was the so-called 'flying Bishop' for Southwark Diocese. He attended Southwark staff meetings and we got on quite well. However there are no 'flying Archdeacons', so I was their Archdeacon whether they liked it or not. On the whole they liked it, and I carried out a two day visit of both parishes.

The most difficult task was to chair the Archdeaconry Pastoral Committee. This was the committee which recommended to the Diocesan Pastoral Committee the churches that should be closed, parishes which should be amalgamated or where team or group ministries formed. It also encouraged churches with unacceptably small congregations to grow so that they were not closed. The committee was elected by the Deaneries, and the Rural Deans and lay chairs were always invited, if not members, when a parish in their Deanery was being discussed.

Some years before, Deaneries had been asked to formulate their own plans for reorganisation, forming cooperative ministries in each area of the Deanery. This had not worked well, mainly because the Deaneries were too near the action to take tough decisions over which churches should be closed.

It was necessary to reduce the number of churches and parishes because the population in South London, though beginning to rise again, was much greater fifty years ago. It was also important that all parishes pulled their weight, as the inner city parishes were being subsidised under the Fairer Shares System. So although every encouragement was given for churches to grow, if they were unable to do so, there came a time when closing a church was the right thing to do. This did not mean fewer people attending overall. In the 17 years I was Archdeacon five churches were closed, but as we have seen, the overall numbers of people attending church still increased.

Closing a church was always very traumatic. I was normally the preacher when these churches were closed, and grown men wept tears of sorrow. All these churches were greatly loved and had seen days when a vibrant ministry took place. However it always happened after years of discussion and debate. Even when a decision to close a church had been taken by the Pastoral Committee, a lengthy legal process under the terms of the Pastoral Measure had to be gone through, before a church was declared redundant. Even then we sometimes had to wait for a Vicar, who held the freehold, to retire before the church could be closed.

Sometimes the Archdeaconry Pastoral Committee did not have to close a church, because the growth plan we insisted on, worked. A remarkable example of this was All Saints Church Camberwell. It was an Evangelical church whose congregation had dropped below the level allowed for an inner city church. The representatives of the church came to the Archdeaconry Pastoral Committee and made a strong case for one more chance.

The Committee was prepared to allow this, so long as they came back with a growth plan that might be successful. This they did, and the committee allowed an appointment to be made of a Deanery Missioner, who would also be Vicar of All Saints Church. Three years later the congregation had grown substantially, so the committee allowed the parish to have a full time Vicar again. The church has since gone from strength to strength and now has a congregation of 500 people.

An experiment which eventually failed, but was still very imaginative and worth trying, was at St Peter Dulwich. This large Victorian church was sold to a Roman Catholic Benedictine Community at Worth Abbey. Some of the monks came to live at St Peter's Vicarage and used the church for worship. The small Anglican congregation continued to worship in the church through a sharing agreement.

For a time this worked well. The monks from Worth enlivened the whole Christian community in Dulwich, including the Anglicans at St Peter's. The latter however never got used to sharing a building, which they did not own, and difficulties arose. These got worse when St Peter's was amalgamated with the next door parish of St Clement's and they had to share a Vicar.

In the end the Abbot decided he had to move the monks back to Worth and sell St Peter's to a Pentecostal church. The Anglicans moved to St Clement's, the other church in the amalgamated parish. This was the pattern which was repeated more than once. Two parishes came together with one Vicar, but keeping two churches and two Parochial Church Councils. For a time this works, but eventually one parish is formed with one church and one Parochial Church Council. Sometimes one church is closed and the other remains open. At others, two churches are closed and a new church built with the proceeds of the sale of both. Three new churches were built in the Archdeaconry when I was Archdeacon.

More costly than building a new church can sometimes be saving an old one. But this is often necessary as some listed churches need to be kept. English Heritage and the Lottery have made it possible to keep churches like St George the Martyr in Southwark, where £3 million is being spent to save the church and provide community facilities in an enlarged crypt. A large amount of money was similarly raised at St Peter's Walworth with an even more imaginative project for community facilities again in the crypt. Over a million pounds was needed to save the St Giles Camberwell spire which dominates the landscape. St James Bermondsey has been transformed but at great expense. Even their unique organ has been restored. St Marys Rotherhithe is visited and helped by Americans because the captain of the Mayflower is buried in the graveyard. All these churches are worth every penny that has been paid, for these prominent and beautiful buildings lift the spirits of all the people in the area. The Archdeaconry Pastoral Committee believed strongly that the inner city greatly needed such buildings.

❧✝❧

CHAPTER 11

Faiths Working Together

M Y work as a Borough Dean continued to be important. By 2000 the
Deans of other denominations were different. David Wade, a very
able black pastor from Camberwell, joined us, as did David Haslam a
Methodist and the National Chair of the Christian Socialists. Simon
Thomas represented the Ichthus Fellowship, a house church group
founded by Roger Forster.

Bruce Stokes, a Baptist, took the lead in persuading the Borough
Deans to found Southwark Churches Care. This proved the churches
could work together on a major project which helped senior citizens to
continue to live in their own homes. Another project helped people with
AIDS. We also prepared for the Millennium. We planned a major
Christian event in Peckham Square in front of the new award winning
library. It was attended by thousands of people and was the first time all
the Christians in the Borough had got together.

In 1999 I was asked to bless the new Thames boat 'Millennium of
Peace' which was owned by a Thames River Company based in
Southwark. This was the boat The Queen sailed in when she went down
the Thames to the Millennium Dome on New Year's Eve to celebrate the
Millennium. I had not realised before that all boats were blessed before
they set sail. There were no prayers for such an event which I could find.
So I had to write my own prayer which I used when I blessed the boat,
filled with London's elite, before her maiden voyage. I prayed as follows:

> Almighty God, creator and sustainer of this good world;
> Before our days began you tamed the seas and hushed its waves.
> Look upon this ship which we bless in your name;
> Ever uphold her with your powerful hand;
> And make calm her path through the waters of the River Thames.
> Your son, the great craftsman, knew the ways of the seas,
> And took pity on his friends amidst the storm,
> We give you thanks for those who designed and built 'Millennium of
>   Peace';

And we pray that by the skill of those who shall sail her, and through
    your good providence,
All may come at length safely to shore.
We ask this in the name of your son, our saviour Jesus Christ. Amen.

    The Borough Deans began to meet with Muslim leaders at this time.
We had tried to do so ten years before but although we met three or four
times, the Muslims called it off saying the time was not ripe. In
Southwark there are not as many Muslims as in other parts of London,
and real local leaders at that time had not emerged. The Imams all came
from outside Southwark and were difficult to contact. This changed after
the Millennium when Professor Dawud Noibi came to live in East
Dulwich and worship at the Old Kent Road mosque.

    Dawud came initially from Egypt. He had an academic background
and was very articulate. He and I got to know one another well and we
began to work closely together. Dawud first formed a Muslim Forum in
Southwark and the Borough Deans started to hold regular meetings with
a few members of the Forum.

    At the same time the government was encouraging Borough Councils
to work in partnership to regenerate inner city areas. They were urged to
form local strategic partnerships which included representatives of
business, education, the police, the local community, and faith groups as
well as the Leader of the Council and Chief Executive. This group of
partners could access money set aside by government to regenerate an
area, provided everyone was genuinely working together on an agreed
plan. The Borough Deans pressed the Leader and Chief Executive
strongly for the representation of Faith communities.

    We were therefore included in the introductory meeting called
'Partnership in Action' at Millwall Football Club. It included all the
major players in the Borough. It was agreed this meeting would meet
each year, leaving a small executive committee to do the work. The
Borough Deans then fought hard for two Faith representatives on the
executive, and we nominated Professor Dawud Noibi and David Wade.
This was accepted.

    It was important however that Dawud Noibi and David Wade had a
representative group to report to and advise them. So a small multi-faith
group was set up to decide what form this should take. I was a member of
the group together with three other Borough Deans, three members of
the Muslim Forum, and one each of the other faith groups in the
Borough who were not so numerous.

We quickly agreed that a Multi-Faith Forum was needed and that two representatives from every church, mosque, synagogue and temple in Southwark should be invited to attend. This meeting would meet once or twice a year and elect the executive committee to meet more often. Dawud Noibi and David Wade should report to this group.

However, before any of this could happen we needed to pay someone to do a lot of work. Even discovering all the churches and faith groups would take time. After this they would have to be contacted and the first meeting of the Multi-Faith Forum arranged.

The Borough Deans fought hard for some of the regeneration money to do this and were successful. The post was advertised and a young Muslim was appointed to do the work. First a list of over 200 churches, mosques, temples, synagogues and other faith groups was put together and the invitations sent out.

The first Southwark Multi-Faith Forum was held in the Damilola Taylor Centre in Peckham. It was a well attended meeting and it elected the executive committee. Simon Hughes gave an inspiring speech. The leaders of all three political parties in the Borough signed a document pledging themselves to consult and work with the Faith communities. They were beginning to realise that this was how they could keep in touch with real grass root communities. There were, however, some Muslim groups which refused to attend, which was perhaps ominous for the future and for their necessary integration into British society. Some Christian churches also failed to attend, and this was not helpful either.

The meetings between the Borough Deans and the Muslim Forum representatives, which included Dawud Noibi, continued to be very important. Trust was built up between us before 9/11, so when that terrible event happened, we were ready to work together to ensure there was no backlash against Muslims in Southwark. We issued joint statements and all the churches worked together to see that Muslim communities in their area were supported.

The same thing happened at the time of the Iraq war. Dawud Noibi knew that he could call me at any time, if anything happened, and I would come immediately. But nothing significant did happen, and this was also true all over London. There is less racism in London than in other parts of the country, particularly the north of England. London can be very proud of the way multi-faith communities work together. Indeed nowhere else do so many different cultures live together in such close proximity. This has resulted in a tolerant and vibrant international community which everyone enjoys. Ken Livingstone has been twice voted Mayor of London because he represents this tolerant, inter-national and multi-cultural London.

The Borough Deans network covered the whole of London and was organised by the London Churches Group. This was the only Christian organisation which spanned London and it was, of course, ecumenical. It occasionally worked together with the Evangelical Alliance, which was nationwide but based in Kennington, South London. A Christian Manifesto was produced during the elections for a Mayor of London. But it was not easy to get agreement among Christians for a really strong line on political issues. I remember sitting on a committee which was drafting a statement on what was needed in London. It was to be signed by the senior Christian leaders, Cardinal Basil Hume, the Bishop of London and Southwark, and the Free Church leaders including some from the Black Led Churches. The first draft we produced was quite strong and would have been worth signing. Subsequent drafts were watered down, and after Cardinal Hume had seen it, watered down still further. In the end it was so anodyne it was not worth producing. I never allowed myself to be involved again.

Nevertheless some things were achieved and one was the London Churches Multi-Faith Major Incident Plan. This was suggested by the then Metropolitan Police Commissioner to Anglican Bishops in London when he met them. I was asked to organise it through the London Churches Group and working with New Scotland Yard.

I had been liasing with New Scotland Yard for the Bishop of Southwark. Latterly I arranged a regular meeting with one of the Assistant Commissioners with representative Archdeacons in London. It was a useful meeting when many things were discussed, including the Stephen Lawrence and Damilola Taylor murders and police chaplains which I had helped to introduce to South London.

The London Churches Multi-Faith Major Incident Plan started with only the Christian churches involved. This was difficult enough to begin with, but four years later all faiths were included and it became a Multi-Faith Plan. It was approved initially by the London Churches Group, and I then worked with the Salvation Army and New Scotland Yard to organise a very large conference at Hendon Police College to launch the plan. Everyone involved was invited and given a copy of the plan. At the conference I explained it and how it would work. I made it clear that it was only a call out plan. Further conferences would be held in each Borough to integrate it with Borough plans and training must happen locally.

At every incident the Salvation Army always send one of their vans to the scene. This would therefore be the headquarters for all clergy called out under the plan. Those who attended the conference were shown the van and the equipment they would be given.

In its final form the plan could be activated by New Scotland Yard, the Salvation Army, the Emergency Planning Officer in a Borough or the local Archdeacon. For the Archdeacons were in command of their own area across London. We called out listed people from the Faith communities who had agreed to do this. These people went to the Salvation Army van at the scene of the incident. They were warned it would be difficult to get through the police cordon, even doctors found this, but they should go to the police control point and insist on getting through. The first person to get to the van took command at the scene, but the Archdeacon remained in overall command. Our job was to visit the scene and see the plan was working, and then see that those who got there first were replaced by others after a reasonable time.

Everyone was warned that a major incident was always chaotic, and that they should use their common sense, when the plan failed to work exactly as laid down. At the Paddington train crash the first clergy on the scene happened to be passing anyway, and they rightly found themselves ministering to the injured and dying, before anyone else got there. Once at the scene, the first clergy person present reports to the relevant police commander and obeys instructions. No person should go to the scene itself without permission. It might be a terrorist attack and therefore unsafe. It is likely also to be a crime scene where forensic and other evidence needs to be taken.

As well as ministering at the scene, assistance could well be required at the temporary mortuary where bodies were identified and relatives needed help. In New York after 9/11 clergy led the bodies out of the disaster area saying prayers. The same thing happened in London after 7/7 2005. The clergy often helped by just being there. The Emergency Services have a dreadful job on such occasions and often need someone to talk to themselves. The police commander at the Paddington train crash told a conference at New Scotland Yard how much he had been helped by one of the clergy who had been present.

Following Hendon, a conference was held every two years at New Scotland Yard to brief the people of all faiths who were involved in the plan, and to make any necessary changes. We would learn from what happened at Paddington, the IRA bombing in the City and Canary Wharf and New York in 2001. Further conferences were held in each

Borough so that people at local level knew one another and were ready to work together. Archdeacons got to know their Borough Emergency Planning officers, and these were also invited to our conferences at New Scotland Yard.

Hospitals of course have their own plans and chaplains to hospitals are part of that. Heathrow also has its own plan, again with the chaplains fully involved. The most difficult task was left to my secretary Meg Johnson. She had the job of keeping the plan up to date. When the plan became 'Multi-Faith', recruitment was difficult, though it became easier with time. It was never easy to prepare people for something which might never happen, or so we hoped. I suspect it is easier since 7/7.

I was a founder member of the Southwark Civic Association. It was composed of the Great and the Good in the Borough. It was independent of the Southwark Borough Council, but the Mayor was the chair, and past mayors remained members for five years. We were the first civic association to give out our own awards to the people of a Borough. Anyone in Southwark could submit names to us for consideration, and we then took time to consider and read the remarkable things which the people of the Borough had done. It was a joy to do this. We so often emphasise the negative and so seldom recognise the good things which are happening.

Rewarding people in this way was greatly appreciated by the people of Southwark, and it helped considerably in promoting community spirit. The awards were made at a ceremony held at Southwark's Roman Catholic cathedral. It was always a packed house, and very moving as the citations for each person were read out and they went up to receive their illuminated scroll.

❧✝❧

CHAPTER 12

The Triumph of Fundamentalism

T H E S E last few years of my ministry were dominated by the challenge of Fundamentalism. This was a worldwide phenomenon. In 1996 a Christian Fundamentalist Eric Rudolph planted a bomb which injured more than 100 people in Centennial Park Atlanta during the 1996 Olympic Games. In 1998 the same Christian Fundamentalist bombed an abortion clinic in Birmingham Alabama, killing a police officer and maiming a nurse. In 2001 Islamic Fundamentalists crashed planes into the World Trade Centre and the Pentagon killing thousands and the world has not been the same since. The damage done by extremist Fundamentalists, whether Muslim or Christian, is obvious, but it is not only the extremists who do harm.

'What do George Bush, the Palestinian Parliament and the Swiss-based Muslim intellectual Tariq Ramadan have in common?' asked Joan Smith in *The Times* on 18th March 2004, she continued:[1]

The answer is that they are all religious conservatives, united in their hostility to homosexuality ... Whether they draw their inspiration from the Bible or the Koran, religious conservatives share the same distaste for gay sex, women's rights and liberal social values of most democracies.

This little noticed consensus undermines the notion, repeated by supporters of Osama Bin Laden after the Madrid bombings, that we are witnessing a twenty-first century replay of the Crusades. That conflict was a clash of religions, Christian versus Muslim . . . what we are seeing now is something very different . . . far from being a conflict between two religions, the motive of the terrorists who have bombed New York, Washington, Bali, Casablanca, Istanbul and Madrid to such horrific effect is the destruction of secular modernity . . . militant religion is the gravest threat to the secular modern world.

Fundamentalism has been around in the United States of America throughout the twentieth century, but it is only since the 1970s that a more politically active type of Fundamentalism has emerged – a Fundamentalism which seeks to rescue the USA from the clutches of secular liberalism and to claim 'dominion' over the social order. It takes a strong and punitive moral line, with a particular stress on homosexuality, pornography, the position of women, and abortion. In 1998 the Southern Baptists declared women should be subservient to the servant leadership of their husband. We are not dealing here with a small minority, but with at least 25% of the American population,[2] with a movement which puts up Fundamentalist presidential candidates and excercised and exercises significant influence on the presidential thinking of both Ronald Reagan and George Bush.

Many Fundamentalists are also Millenarianists who follow closely the Scofield Reference Bible written in 1909. According to Scofield and another divine, John Nelson Darby, God has divided history into seven-year plans or dispensations. During each dispensation, God relates to a man in a different way. During the last but one dispensation, Christ will defeat the anti-christ at Armageddon, fifty five miles north of Tel Aviv. Just before the battle, the church will be wafted to heaven and all the good people will experience 'rapture', as Scofield calls it. The wicked will suffer horribly. Then after seven years of 'burying the dead', God returns bringing peace, joy and the raptured ones.[3]

This gospel has been preached daily by American television divines. In 1984 39% of the American people believed in the death of Earth by nuclear fire and rapture. Among the 39% was Ronald Reagan.[4]

Such prophecy is particularly important in determining American attitudes to Israel and to nuclear war.[5]

Ideas of millenarian disaster, says community theologian Ken Leech, were reflected in the speeches of Ronald Reagan – while Pat Robertson, who stood for the presidency, has worked out his narrative in terms of a global millennial apocalypse. 'Armageddon theology' has played a key role in American foreign policy, and it is not inconceivable that it could do so again. It is a matter of the utmost urgency that we recognise how influential Fundamentalism and Millenarianism are in American life. We are not dealing with a lunatic fringe but with a mass movement involving very large numbers of people.

President George Bush is a Fundamentalist from this stable and is more of a committed Evangelical than Ronald Reagan. The Conservative Evangelicals who were largely responsible for getting him elected see him as 'one of them'. Reagan was never seen in this light, but Bush is expected to deliver on the Fundamentalist agenda. He has already announced his intention of changing the United States Constitution to outlaw gay marriage, and is expected to ensure a conservative majority on the

Supreme Court so that current laws on abortion and school prayers can be changed.

The clearest sign of a Christian, and, more specifically, Evangelical influence on Bush's ethics is his repeated invocation of the conflict between Good and Evil, says Peter Singer in his book *The President of Good and Evil*.[6]

Bush urges us to call 'Evil by its name' to 'fight Evil' and tells us that out of Evil will come Good. This language comes straight out of apocalyptic Christianity. To understand the context in which Bush uses this language, we need to remember that tens of millions of Americans hold an apocalyptic view of the world. According to a poll taken by *Time*,[7] 53% of adult Americans 'expect the imminent return of Jesus Christ, accompanied by the fulfilment of biblical prophecies concerning the cataclysmic destruction of all that is wicked'

Projecting this prophecy on to the world in which they live, many American Christians see their own nation as carrying out a divine mission. The Nation's enemies therefore are demonised. That is exactly what Bush does. During a discussion about the looming Iraq war with Australian Prime Minister John Howard in February 2003, Bush said that liberty for the people of Iraq would not be a gift that the United States could provide, but rather 'God's gift to every human being in the world'.[8]

Michael Gerson,[9] who had overall responsibility for the Axis of Evil speech, is an Evangelical Christian. He changed 'axis of hatred' to 'axis of evil' because he wanted to use the theological language that Bush had made his own since 9/11. Don Evans,[10] who is not only Bush's commerce secretary but also a close friend, says that Bush's religious faith gives him 'a very clear sense of what is Good and what is Evil.'

In comparing the rhetoric of George Bush and Osama bin Laden with regard to 9/11, theologian Bruce Lincoln found far more in common than one might expect. 'Both men constructed a Manichaean struggle,' he writes in *Holy Terrors*, 'where Sons of Light confront Sons of Darkness, and all must enlist on one side or another, without possibility of neutrality, hesitation, or middle ground.'[11]

Esther Kaplan, in her book *With God On Their Side*, shows that President Bush devoted much of his first term to cultivating the support of his fellow Christian Fundamentalists. Family planning and AIDS organisations saw their funds cut, while church groups received millions of dollars to promote sexual abstinence and marriage. This has made easier the administration's relentless efforts to upend the Nation's tax system to serve an economic elite and dismantle what remains of the welfare state. Esther Kaplan writes,[12]

But these 'revolutionary' changes to benefit the few at the expense of the many, have only been made possible by efforts to keep the administration's Christian right base not only appeased, or even satisfied, but inflamed.

Just as Israel's Likud Party is in thrall to ultra-orthodox settlers who are convinced the occupied territories were given to them by God, as India's former prime minister Atal Bihari Vajpayee found it politically necessary to support the violent Hindu nationalism of his party's religious followers, as Egypt and other moderate governments in the Arab World must tread carefully in the face of growing Muslim Fundamentalism, so our governing Republican Party is unmistakably in the grips of its own Christian theocratic base.

All over the world Fundamentalism is gaining strength. When Tariq Ali[13] grew up in Lahore in Pakistan, he and most of his friends were atheists. His parents too were non-believers. So were most of their close friends. In *The Clash of Fundamentalisms* he writes,

In the second half of the last century, a large proportion of educated Muslims had embraced modernity. They realised that organised religion was an anachronism. Old habits persisted, nonetheless: The would-be virtuous made their ablutions and sloped off sheepishly to Friday prayers. Sometimes they fasted for a few days each year, usually just before the new moon was sighted, marking the end of Ramadan. I doubt whether more than a quarter of the population in the cities fasted for a whole month . . . Mullahs, especially the rural variety, were objects of ridicule, widely regarded as dishonest, hypocritical and lazy.

As the years progressed, Pakistan regressed. The study of Islam was made compulsory in the late seventies. In the 1980s and 1990s Pakistan helped to give birth to the Taleban, and to the Madrassa schools. The Taleban creed is a variant of the Deobandi Islam professed by a sectarian strain in Pakistan. The Taleban, when they gained power in Afghanistan, banned women from working, collecting their children from school and in some cities even shopping, effectively confining them to their homes. Girl's schools were closed down. The Taleban had been taught in the Madrassas to steer clear of the temptation of women. Male brotherhood was a condition of tight military discipline. Puritanism extended to snuffing out sexual expression of any kind; although this was a region where homosexual practices had been common for centuries, recruits guilty of the crime were executed by Taleban commanders. Similar stories could be told of Iran and the Sudan where Fundamentalists have gained control.

But even some moderate Muslims are Fundamentalists and advocate a degree of control over everyday life, including a type of sexual segregation that secular societies find completely unacceptable. Tariq Ramadan[14] for instance has advised Muslims not to shake hands with a member of the opposite sex or to take part in mixed sports. Other Muslim thinkers such as Dalil Boubakeur,[15] president of the French Council of the Muslim Religion and certainly not considered an extremist, quoted the prophet's observation that when a man and woman find themselves alone, the Devil will be their companion.

One of the most popular texts in Muslim bookshops *La Voie de Musulman* by Saudi cleric Aboubakr Eldjazairi[16] declares 'The woman must stay in the family home, and not leave it, without the permission of her husband. If she goes out, she is required to lower her gaze not to cause harm, and not to become involved in coarse or indecent conversation.'

Homosexuality in all Muslim countries is treated harshly, especially in Iran and countries like Nigeria where Muslim and Christian Fundamentalists have the same attitude to gay people, and where attempts are made to introduce Sharia law even when Christians are present. Three hundred gay Palestinians are believed to have sought refuge in Tel Aviv, the Israeli city with a flourishing gay culture, to escape beatings and torture at home. In Jerusalem, Christians and Muslims combined to prevent a Gay Pride March. Indeed Conservative Evangelical Christians are realising more and more that as Fundamentalists they are on the same side of the argument as their fellow Muslim Fundamentalists. The first reaction of some Fundamentalist Evangelists in the United States to the 9/11 hits explained that they were 'God's punishment for the sin of tolerating homosexuality and abortion.' Al Quaeda would of course agree.[17]

In the last years of my ministry none of this could be ignored. Religion was increasingly seen as the problem. The burning of Salman Rushdie's book *The Satanic Verses* in Bradford in the 1980s should have been a warning. Soon afterwards women Muslims I knew started to cover their heads when they had never bothered to do so before. IRA bombs continued to go off throughout the country and reminded people of extremist religion in Ireland and the harm that it does. Then in 1998 people watched in disbelief on their television screens as a Fundamentalist Anglican African Bishop attending the Lambeth Conference, screaming that Leviticus called for the death penalty against homosexuals, attempted unsuccessfully to exorcise the gayness from Richard Kirker, the leader of the Lesbian and Gay Christian Movement.

He was one of many Fundamentalist Anglican Bishops who dominated the 1998 Lambeth Conference resulting, with the help of Archbishop George Carey, in the conference taking what was seen as a strong anti-gay line. People in London who believed in equal opportunities and accepted homosexuality were appalled. People were particularly shocked that the Anglican church, which most people see as reasonable and not extremist, was acting in such an unreasonable way. Both Christian and non-Christian people were equally appalled. Many felt this showed that religion was indeed a problem and doing positive harm. Nevertheless it was a considerable victory for Fundamentalism. But how had it come about?

The Churches of the Anglican Communion were mostly founded by those who brought the British Empire into being. Wherever the British went they took with them Anglicanism and especially Anglican missionaries. The trouble was that more of them came from the Evangelical missionary societies than the Catholic ones. The Evangelical missionaries were also mostly Fundamentalist, and went to countries like Pakistan and Nigeria where they had to compete, especially in recent years, with Fundamentalist Muslims. The agenda, therefore, for some Anglican Bishops at Lambeth was partly set by the influence of a strong Fundamentalist Muslim culture, which just could not accept homosexuality, and which put great pressure on the Bishops to be equally dismissive of homosexuality.

But it was also clear that Fundamentalist Evangelicals in England realised they could strengthen their position by the support of such Bishops abroad. In February 1997 therefore, 80 Anglican Bishops from the developing world, assisted by Conservative Evangelicals in England, met in Kuala Lumpur[18] to prepare for Lambeth and issued a conservative statement. They said, 'The Holy Scriptures are clear in teaching that all sexual promiscuity is sin. We are convinced that this includes homosexual practices between men or women as well as heterosexual practices outside marriage.'

The English Evangelical Primate of the 'Southern Zone' was also active. This enormous Anglican province stretches from Peru to Tierra del Fuego in South America. His province only has 22,000 members so he had plenty of time to campaign on this issue. Gregory Venables in particular, when he held the post, spent a lot of time in England telling the rest of us what to do.

In September 1997 English Conservative Evangelicals from the Oxford Centre for Mission studies, whose leaders would claim for themselves an increasing role in coordinating international opposition on the gay issue in the years ahead, met 50 Bishops largely from Africa in Dallas,[19] home of one of the most conservative of the United States Bishops. They declared that there was a socio-political campaign to promote homosexuality within the Church and they would not permit it.

Not all African Bishops however opposed homosexuality. The South African Church had been brought into being through Anglo-Catholic missionaries, not least the monks from the Community of the Resurrection at Mirfield. They had also suffered from Apartheid and opposed it strongly and successfully. Another kind of Apartheid should, they thought, also be opposed. Archbishop Desmond Tutu had this to say:[20]

It is a matter of ordinary justice. We struggled against Apartheid in South Africa because we were blamed and made to suffer for something we could do nothing about. This is the same with homosexuality. The orientation is given, not a matter of choice. It would be crazy for someone to chose to be gay, given the homophobia that is present . . . our Anglican church says that orientation is okay, but gay sex activity is wrong. That is crazy.

However the Lambeth Bishops did not listen. This would not have mattered too much if they had been prepared to allow provinces, like the Episcopal Church in the United States of America or the Anglican Church in Canada, working in a different culture from that of Africa, to have a different opinion. At the 1988 Lambeth Conference the Bishops of the West allowed this argument for the Africans over polygamy when African Bishops pleaded that some notice be taken of their different culture. In 1998 the African Bishops were not prepared to do the same.

The inevitable result was that the Episcopal Church in the United States and the Anglican Church of Canada went ahead anyway. This they were perfectly entitled to do as all provinces in the Anglican Communion are autonomous. It greatly cheered those I knew in London who were devastated by the actions of Archbishop George Carey and most of the other English Bishops at the Lambeth Conference.

The Anglican Church in the United States was able to approve the consecration of the first openly gay Anglican Bishop partly because it had very few Evangelicals. The American Church was much closer to the ethos of the Church of England in the 1940s and 1950s when Conservative Evangelicals had little say in decision making.

Fundamentalist Evangelicals worldwide were nonetheless enraged by the consecration of Gene Robinson as Bishop of New Hampshire. But so too were liberal people in Britain by Archbishop Rowan Williams forcing Jeffrey John to stand down from being Bishop of Reading. This led to two important interventions by African Bishops. The first should have been listened to by the English Bishops, but to their shame they ignored it.

Archbishop Ndungane of South Africa laid into his fellow African Primates in an interview for the *Guardian*:[21]

There is an attempt to divert us from the major life and death issues in the world. There is a woman waiting to be stoned to death for adultery in Nigeria and yet we are not hearing any fuss from the leadership of the Church there about that . . . It is very arrogant to assume that the people in America do not know what they are doing. We have got to respect their decision. We have also got to respect the integrity of our provinces as autonomous entities whether we agree with them or not, or whether they make us uncomfortable or not . . . Some kind of hypocrisy is going on in the Church. Gene Robinson and Jeffrey John have been open and honest about their private lives. It is no secret that there are gay clergy and there are gay Bishops and the institutional Church seems to be turning a blind eye when we should be encouraging honesty. If Gene Robinson had kept quiet there would have been no issue.

I know people who are gay and lesbian who are African. The issue of orientation knows no culture and my fellow bishops are in denial, they have an ostrich mentality on this subject. Our church must learn how to live together as a diverse community. That's what should be on the agenda, not seeking to cast stones or talking about schism.

If only English Bishops could talk like that! Instead the majority sided more with Archbishop Peter Akinola of Nigeria, the same Archbishop who had not made any fuss about the woman waiting to be stoned in his own country. He said in the *Church Times*:[22]

Homosexuality is flagrant disobedience to God, which enables people to pervert God's ordained sexual expression with the opposite sex. In this way homosexuals have missed the mark; they have shown themselves to be trespassers of God's divine laws.

The practice of homosexuality in our understanding of scripture is the enthronement of self-will and human weakness and a rejection of God's order and will. This cannot be treated with levity; otherwise the Church, and the God she preaches, will be badly deformed and diminished.

The acceptance of homosexuality and lesbianism as normal is the triumph of disobedience; the enthronement of human pride over the will of God. This lifestyle is a terrible violation of the harmony of the eco-system of which mankind is a part. As we are rightly concerned by the depletion of the ozone layer, so we should be concerned by the practice of homosexuality.

God instituted marriage between man and woman, among other reasons for procreation. To set aside this divine arrangement in preference to self-centred perversion, is an assault on the sovereignty of God. Homosexuality is an abuse of man's body just as much as lesbianism is . . . God created two persons – male and female. Now the world of homosexuals has created a third – a homosexual, neither male nor female or both male and female – a strange two in-one human . . . homosexuality or lesbianism or bestiality is to us a form of slavery and redemption from it is readily available through repentance and faith in the saving grace of our Lord Jesus Christ.

The Nigerian Muslims who, under Sharia law, had sentenced a young woman to be stoned would have agreed. It was stranger to see some English Bishops side more with Archbishop Akinola than Archbishop Ndungane. They were content to overlook the shortcomings of the Church in Central Africa. The Bishop of Durham Tom Wright, the Church's leading Evangelical, said in the *Independent*,[23] 'There is an implicit sense that we in North-West Europe and America actually know how the world works and you poor people have to catch up. Those who enshrine tolerance become extremely intolerant of anyone who disagrees.' But this was not so, as Stephen Bates[24] of the *Guardian* has pointed out, 'No one in the decadent West was attempting to assert that Africans should start electing gay Bishops.'

The Bishop of Durham and other English Bishops failed to back the views of African Bishops in South Africa. Were these not Africans too? Were Archbishop Ndungane and Archbishop Desmond Tutu not worth listening to? Most people I know believe Archbishop Desmond Tutu and his successor are more likely to be right than these English Bishops or the Archbishop of Nigeria.

I have gone into some detail because in my last years as Archdeacon of Southwark it dominated the discussion I had with many people. This was not just the clergy and lay people in the parish, but secular people in London who I worked with. They could not understand why the Church was allowing itself to look so ridiculous. Homosexuality had been accepted by them for years, and Councillors on the London Borough of Southwark were strong in advocating equal opportunities for all, and ensuring that no discrimination took place against women, black and Asian people and gays and lesbians. Yet here was the Anglican Church advocating discrimination against gay clergy. It made mission very difficult. I did not want to evangelise only homophobic people. We had enough of those in the Church already.

It was also a huge disappointment that Archbishop Rowan Williams was making things worse. His treatment of Jeffrey John played into the hands of the Fundamentalists. From then on they knew they had him on the run. He persuaded his fellow Primates to set up the Eames Commission to make recommendations as to how best the Anglican Communion might tackle 'grave difficulties'. But this only resulted in a further victory for Archbishop Akinola, when the Episcopal Church in the United States of America and the Canadian Anglican Church were required to repent and forced to exclude themselves from the Primates meeting and the Anglican Consultative Council. Everyone is expecting Archbishop Akinola will soon win an even greater victory for Fundamentalists, by driving the Episcopal Church in the United States of America and the Canadian Anglican Church out of the Anglican Communion. Even if the American churches back down for a time – this may not be enough to keep the Communion together.

Archbishop Rowan Williams seems more concerned to appease the Fundamentalists and keep the Anglican Communion together, than to stand up for the truth. The price being paid is however, too great. It was summed up in General Synod by Brian McHenry[25] who was a member of the Archbishop's Council, and a Reader I knew well in the Southwark Archdeaconry. He said 'There is increasing evidence that we are not in tune with public opinion. It is uncomfortable to be a member of a Church which is perceived to be homophobic, hypocritical and discriminatory.'

I returned to Shrewsbury in January 2004. I was glad to do so. The Church of England was no longer the tolerant, moderate and broad church which I knew when last in Shrewsbury 40 years before. I went back to Southwark once more in May to receive the honorary Freedom of the Borough of Southwark. This was an award made by Southwark Borough Council, and I was particularly pleased to be given such an honour by a secular body in a Borough where I had worked so happily for so long.

Most of the family were now back in Shropshire, Marion returned first with her husband, John Jones, who was an ICI executive. My brother, Allan, came back with his wife Mary (nee Jones). He retired from Ready Mixed Concrete when he was Managing Director of the U. K. Company. He subsequently became Chair of the North Shropshire Conservatives. Cynthia never left Shrewsbury, where she was a teacher and married to the Reverend David Uffindell, who was an Engineer and a Non-Stipendiary Priest at Harlescott Parish Church. Susan was the only sibling who did not now live in Salop. She continued to live in Somerset with her husband, Guy Boddington, where she organised educational trips for French schoolchildren.

The Town of Shrewsbury was little changed, but the religious scene was different. St Mary's Church where I worshipped when young was now redundant, though kept beautifully by the Churches Conservation Trust. One Sung Eucharist a year is still allowed and I have preached at this service. Indeed I also celebrated and preached at the first Eucharist held there after it was declared redundant. Six other services are held each year as well as concerts and exhibitions. The spire of the church built on the highest hill in Shrewsbury still dominates the town, but the redundancy of such a prominent and historic church sends out a very negative signal to the residents of the town.

The church was made redundant because of a recommendation in the Salop Archdeaconry report of 1981.[26] There was a policy decision to close the town centre churches except for St Chad's. This was because 'the old churches are clustered together in the centre of town whereas the main growth of Shrewsbury has been on the periphery.' St Julian's was closed in 1976, a thriving Evangelical church which it was even more foolish to close. It is still used by Evangelicals for worship but they are not members of the Church of England. The policy was wrong because the churches in the centre of town are prominent, historic and people know where they are and how to get to them, whereas the churches on the periphery are mostly uninteresting, small and difficult to find. Little can be done about this now, and the present Bishop, Archdeacon and clergy were not around when the decisions were made.

My father and mother contributed to the decline of St Mary's by leaving long before it was made redundant. In 1969 the Reverend Henry Follis was appointed Vicar, and introduced Mattins. This was too much for father, and from then on, he and my mother, worshipped at All Saints Church Castlefields, the most Anglo-Catholic church in Shrewsbury. They were not alone in leaving at this time, and though the Sung Eucharist was eventually restored, they never returned. The altar, now used at All Saints' to celebrate Mass, was given by the family in memory of my father. It was therefore the obvious church to attend when we returned to Shrewsbury. However, the Church Council is at present against the ordination of women to the priesthood, and has opted for the extended Episcopal care of the flying Bishop, so although I have worshipped there occasionally, it cannot be my spiritual home.

The other big difference is the strength of the Evangelicals. This mirrors what has happened in the Church of England as a whole. Evangelical vicars are now in position at five parish churches in Shrewsbury, though not all have Evangelical congregations. St Chad's Church is now almost the only liberal catholic church. The Vicar, Mark Thomas, has a good relationship with the Civic Authorities and town Councillors. He has introduced a yearly Darwin Lecture as part of the town's Darwin Festival. Charles Darwin was born in the town and went to Shrewsbury School. A lecture which shows how evolution is compatible with Christianity is important, especially as some of the local Evangelicals support creationism. St Chad's is the church I now attend and help out at sometimes. It is well attended and shows that Liberal Catholicism can still be successful.

I remain a Chaplain to the Queen until the age of seventy and still go to London to preach at the Chapel Royal. I am also on the Executive Committee of the Shrewsbury Housing Forum which was founded with the help of Bishop Ronnie Bowlby, who also now lives in Shrewsbury, and is still President of the Forum. I continue therefore to press for much needed low cost housing which is needed in Shrewsbury as elsewhere.

I have resumed my regular support for Shrewsbury Town Football Club. I go to most home games. They had sunk to the Conference when I returned to Shrewsbury, but went straight back into the League the following season. They are building a new stadium to house their 5,000 or so hard core supporters. It will hold 10,000 on big occasions.

My wife Ann continues to work part-time as an Occupational Therapist. She has redesigned and transformed our garden in Shrewsbury and made it better than the London garden. She is a member of the Shropshire Organic Gardeners and through them she opened our garden to visitors only 18 months after we arrived from London.

I have rejoined the Lion Club, though it no longer meets at the Lion, which is not the Inn it once was. Laurence Le Quesne is the only member remaining from the 1950s and 60s. Those who come are still mostly teachers at Shrewsbury School and we meet now at the Admiral Benbow. We occasionally remind the current members that it was started by Frank McEachran in the 1930s for discussion over a good glass of beer.

Some of our members recently saw *The History Boys* by Alan Bennett and it was thought that Hector had some of Kek's characteristics. In 2005

Alan Bennett was written to, and he confirmed that this was deliberate. He wrote:[27]

I'd long wanted to write about a charismatic schoolmaster. I was first told about McEachran by John Ryle, a friend who was taught by him at Shrewsbury. He put me onto the books of spells and sent me the obituary from the school magazine. I talked to Paul Foot about him, not long before Paul's death and also to Michael Palin, who knew of him by repute. Hector is not a portrait of Kek of course. He is a figure of myth, whose misdemeanours in the play lead to a downfall rather more sensational than Kek's demise. But the 'spells' in *The History Boys* remain the heartbeat of the play. 'They're learned by heart,' says Hector, 'and that is where they belong.'

We have often discussed over real ale some of the themes in this book. My lack of regard for Evangelical Fundamentalists is well known. So are my positive feelings for the Church of England, and what we might achieve if only we can stand up to the Fundamentalists.

I have often argued there is as much need for Christian leaders to challenge Fundamentalism within Christianity, as there is for Muslim leaders to do so within Islam. For, as we have seen in this chapter, Religious Fundamentalism, of all kinds, does great harm. In January 2006 Professor Richard Dawkins on Channel 4 Television asked if Religion was the root of all evil. It is not that, and true religion is responsible for much good in the world, but Fundamentalism is indeed the root of much Evil.

❧✝❧

CHAPTER 13

Fighting Fundamentalism

THE London bombs have made people even more worried about Religious Fundamentalism. It is clear that many Muslims are as counter cultural as many Conservative Evangelicals would have us be. They hate the culture in which they have been brought up. 31% of Muslims who were polled in a *Telegraph* YouGov poll[1] shortly after the London bombs exploded agreed with the statement: 'Western democracy is decadent and immoral and Muslims should seek to bring it to an end but only by non violent means.'

David Banting,[2] Chair of Reform, is not saying anything very different when he adds: 'We are moving into a world where the Church is going to have to be counter cultural, more so than it has been for a thousand years.' Stephen Bates[3] the *Guardian* journalist warns that 'Just as the Militant Tendency tried to subvert the old Labour Party in the 1980s, so the Church of England is being invaded by a Taleban Tendency with its own agenda and strong determination to win. This is a takeover bid, to create a pure church of only one sort of believer. And it has found allies in the USA and the developing world.'

Stephen Pritchard[4] writing in the *Observer* agrees with this and adds: 'What the Evangelicals cannot grasp is that their self-righteous crusade against a tiny minority is driving away thinking heterosexuals, disgusted at their tactics and dismayed that the Church's leadership is so supine'. Finally Joan Smith[5] writing in *The Times* said that she and her friends saw that 'Militant religion is the gravest threat to the secular modern world . . . Individual freedom depends on keeping religion firmly in its place.'

We need to take these words very seriously and fight to keep the Church of England tolerant and sensible even if this means ditching the Anglican Communion. We need to remember how we became a Church in the sixteenth century. For the Elizabethan Settlement was formed in not dissimilar circumstances to today.

Elizabeth I stood for the *Via Media*. The extremes of Roman Catholicism and the Puritans (the Evangelicals of the time) were not part of the Established Church. Elizabeth tolerated Catholics and Puritans who were loyal. But she knew that both posed a danger to the State and the Church. The Pope issued a 'fatwa' excommunicating Elizabeth and encouraging Catholics to kill her. The Puritans were already stirring up trouble, which would lead in the end to the beheading of Charles I, and the establishment of the Commonwealth under Oliver Cromwell – a society which even extremist Muslims would not find decadent.

The Church of England in Elizabeth's time was still a very broad Church. From those who wanted to keep Bishops, the Sacraments and some Catholic practices to those who were moderate Puritans. From time to time some people attempted to make the Church more Puritan, but Elizabeth insisted on moderation and pounced on extremists.

Members of the Church of England need to remember this today. No one wants the Conservative Evangelicals to give up their beliefs, but they must allow others to keep theirs, and this they are not doing at present. There would be no problem over homosexuals for instance, if the Conservative Evangelicals allowed the Liberals to hold their view, whilst they held to theirs. This would seem the sensible thing to do, over an issue which many believe to be secondary, when compared with the main doctrines of the Church. It already happens over the ordination of women to the priesthood where 'two integrities' have been agreed. But the Conservative Evangelicals refuse to do this because for them it is a major issue as scripture they believe says homosexuality is wrong. Therefore to accept homosexuality is to deny scripture.

This is a pretty dubious argument for many reasons. The Bible is not clear on the issue. Jesus says nothing against homosexuality. Paul is against homosexual promiscuity, but says and knows nothing of homosexual partnerships which are not promiscuous. There are a few verses in the Old Testament which condemn homosexuality but many more which condemn usury, and I don't know of many Evangelicals who refuse to take interest from a bank. Scripture has not prevented Evangelicals being against slavery – though many opposed Wilberforce at the time of abolition. Most Evangelicals have been able to support women priests; so what is the problem over homosexuality? It seems we only have homophobia left as a reason.

But there is no doubt many Conservative Evangelicals view the Bible differently from others – not least from the way I have used the Bible in this book. They believe in the verbal inspiration and sole authority of scripture. They treat the Bible like Muslims treat the Koran (Qur'an).

They are in fact Fundamentalists. They ignore what has been Anglican teaching since Elizabethan times, when the theologian Richard Hooker formulated the classic Anglican position which called for reliance not just on 'scripture', but also on 'tradition' meaning the whole inspired experience of the Church of Christ, and on 'reason' as the God given glory of humanity. All three must be used if we are to get at the truth. Fundamentalists rely only on one. But it is the lack of any real 'authority' being given to 'reason' which causes the harm.

The debate about homosexuality therefore has become the defining moment for many Conservative Evangelicals who only rely on scripture. Wallace Benn the Bishop of Lewes makes this very clear:[6]

I think homosexuality is the presenting issue of a much deeper problem, which is how faithful to the teaching of the Bible will the Church be? It teaches us God's perspective on how he made us and how we are meant to relate to one another sexually. Jesus offers forgiveness and a new way of life. If the gospel says believe in Christ, if I change what it says, I change the Bible. Homosexuality has become the key. I wish it wasn't, but it has become the issue we are presented with.

Many believe that Conservative Evangelicals have chosen this ground in order to take over the Church of England. Christina Rees, who has served on the Archbishop's Council and is a liberal Evangelical, believes this to be the case:[7]

Conservative Evangelicals want to govern the institution of the Church and all its boards and councils. That is their avowed aim. They want to end up running the whole Church, to make theirs the dominant view . . . Cultural imperialism is now coming from the developing world. Just as it is wrong for Victorian missionaries to cover up nudity among Africans in the nineteenth century, we are now being told that we are wrong and that we have to live in a certain way. That doesn't make it right. We have learned to treat other cultures with respect but what is clear is that when some Anglicans speak out on the issue now, it comes with a threat.

I think it is about how men see themselves. It is about a cultural under-standing of manhood and masculinity. It is anathema to men to think of not being very heterosexual. In Africa there is no concept of sexual orientation as there is in the West. Things which threaten the patriarchy will not be tolerated.

The likely strength of Conservative Evangelicalism in the future can be seen in some universities. We are rightly worried about universities as a breeding ground for Muslim Fundamentalists. We should worry also about Fundamentalist Christians. In September 1999 the *Guardian* reported their huge success at the University of Durham where the

Evangelical Christian Union is the biggest university society with 500 members. Jonathan Margolis believes that Christianity may be becoming the 'symptom of youth rebellion[8] – a novel counter-culture for students.' One student, hitherto a churchgoer, expresses her concern at what is going on in what she describes as 'in your face' religion:

It very soon became obvious that it was not only Evangelical, but very Orthodox and Fundamentalist with elements of racism, sexism and homophobia.

What is striking is the conservative interpretation of the Bible, with a narrow view of morals that ignores, for example, consumerism, and does not prevent these students from moving to take well-paid jobs with vast multinational conglomerates with little moral concern for the parts of the world they exploit.

The prospect of a flood of hardline religious zealots emerging from Britain's universities who see other Christians as simply wrongheaded is no more encouraging than the Fundamentalist views of some Muslim youths. The dangers of growing Fundamentalism here, especially if it becomes politically useful, as it now is to politicians in America, is obvious.

There is the prospect also of Christians and Muslim Fundamentalists working together to change society towards the goals they share. David Banting, the leader of Reform in the Church of England, told Stephen Bates of the *Guardian*, that one of the things he had learned from networking with Muslims in his former parish in Oldham was that they cannot understand a Church where people can question the faith.[9] 'I learned not to be frightened of clear Christian convictions. There was a huge common ground on social and moral issues with the Muslims. We had solidarity.' The truth of this became clear in January 2006 when Sir Iqbal Sacranie, the head of the Muslim Council of Britain, told BBC Radio 4 listeners that same-sex relationships risked damaging the foundations of society, and scientific evidence showed that homosexuality carried high health risks.[10]

Each of our Faiths tells us that it is harmful and, I think, if you look into the scientific evidence that has been available in terms of the forms of various illnesses and diseases that are there, surely it points out that where homosexuality is practised there is a greater concern in that area.

Such a medieval view is swimming against the tide of public opinion. Most of us would prefer Britain as it is, grounded in the toleration of the Elizabethan Settlement and the Enlightenment. We are proud of British democracy, and far from seeing the West as decadent, we see it as a place of freedom of thought for people of all sorts and where we can still question religious faith. We are against racism, sexism, anti-Semitism and homophobia. We are glad we are no longer subject to religious prohibition on extra marital sex, abortion, homosexuality and contraception. The findings of science and evolution are accepted and therefore taught in schools.

We also enjoy excellent films like *The Life of Brian* or good books like Salmon Rushdie's *The Satanic Verses*. The Church of England as the Established Church should be supportive of such a society and stamp on religious extremism which tries to turn the clock back. For the Church of England was formed by the Elizabethan Settlement of toleration and the avoidance of extremes. Today we need such a Church more than ever.

Since 1990 there has been a surge of books on the Quest for the historical Jesus, with the time, place and social setting of Jesus, newly illuminated by renewed and vigorous investigation of the Dead Sea Scrolls and other Jewish and Hellenistic sources. The encouraging outcome has been that even radical writers like John Dominic Crossan and Marcus Borg believe more can be known about the historical Jesus than used to be the case forty years ago.

This research has proved that the historical Jesus spent most of his time with the outcasts of his day, the poor, the tax gatherers, the lepers and sinners. I have no doubt that today gay people would be included. His condemnation would be equally clear. He condemned the Pharisees in his own day. He would also condemn today's Pharisees. As Christina Rees has rightly said:[11]

The most important thing is that nowhere in the life and ministry of Jesus Christ does he ever mention the issue of homosexuality, not one word. If Conservative Evangelicals want to make the gay issue a line in the sand they are doing something our Lord did not. They are elevating the issue into a Christian orthodoxy and that is very misguided.

If you look into the core message it is one of overwhelming unconditional love of God. God wants all of creation to be reconciled to Him. That message is rather more important. Jesus was ridiculed for associating with down and outs and outcasts and reserved most of his ridicule for the hierarchy; Woe unto you, you hypocrites. That was said to the religious hierarchy of his day. I really think we should ask ourselves, who would Jesus be spending time with now and what would he be saying?

The Holy Spirit is trying to tell us the answer. She is the one which scripture says will lead us into all truth. She does not just speak through

Christians; indeed she probably finds this very difficult. She is however speaking loud and clear through many people in this country who have accepted gay people long ago. This includes all the main political parties. For under David Cameron, even the Conservative Party is now more supportive of gay people than the Church of England. She is speaking through the Episcopal Church in the United States of America when consecrating an openly gay bishop, and through the Canadian Anglican Church when allowing 'same sex' blessings.

These two provinces in the Anglican Communion are shining lights which need our support against their Fundamentalist opponents. We must side strongly with them and make this clear in any way we can. We must listen to Archbishop Winston Ndungane of South Africa rather than Archbishop Peter Akinola of Nigeria. If the Anglican Funda- mentalist Bishops threaten to wreck the Anglican Communion, we should let them do it, rather than give way to their demands. The Anglican Communion is only worth saving if the Fundamentalists are not in control and the American and Canadian Churches are part of it. For there is much at stake here. The Church of England will only be credible intellectually in the future, if it sides with the forces of reason.

A strong attempt should nevertheless still be made to allow each province the autonomy they have always had in the past. No one wants to force the Province of Nigeria to accept homosexuals. We want them to change their minds of course, but we accept they have a perfect right as an autonomous province to their point of view. All we ask is that they and others allow the Episcopal Church in the United States and the Anglican Church of Canada the same right. But if the American and Canadian Churches are expelled, then the Church of England must side with them and not the Fundamentalists. We must side with those Christians who value the Enlightenment and are not afraid of modern life.

The Archbishop of Canterbury and the English Bishops must oppose Fundamentalism. They must stand up and be counted as Neil Kinnock did when he opposed the Militant Tendency in the Labour Party. As Bishops of the Established Church they must speak for the 72% of Christians in this country who claimed to be Christian in the census, rather than the small percentage of Conservative Evangelicals who go to church. If they cannot do this, then the rest of us must oppose them for the sake of the future of the Church.

Parishes and individual Anglicans must make it clear to the Bishops that they are staying in communion with the Episcopal Church in the

United States and the Anglican Church of Canada, regardless of anything the Bishops may say. Parochial Church Councils should pass resolutions making this clear. Priests and lay people from the American and Canadian churches should be invited to England so that their priests can celebrate and preach in our churches. We should ignore any attempt by the Bishops to stop this. We should encourage people to wear a badge indicating that they are still in communion with these Churches.

We should also do what we can to ensure the clergy freehold is kept. Most Bishops, as we have seen, are unable to stand up to the Fundamentalists. Therefore the clergy still need the protection of the freehold. They can then continue their own lifestyle and refuse to answer impertinent questions about sex. Their churches can also stay in communion with the American and Canadian churches.

We should continue to support the Establishment of the Church for it has a moderating influence on the Bishops and the Evangelicals. They might talk a lot about being counter-cultural, but in practice many want to be part of mainstream British society rather than a Fundamentalist sect outside the Establishment. Furthermore those in the mainstream of society are increasingly active in support of the Church. A recent opinion poll, carried out by ORB,[12] suggests that 43% of the adult population attended Church at Christmas 2005. This is 10% more than in 2001. These are the people we need to listen to and support, not a minority of Conservative Evangelicals.

We should also work closely with the Methodist Church and continue to seek unity with them. There are fewer Evangelicals in the Methodist Church and a strong liberal tradition. So any United Church is going to have more Liberals in it than the Church of England has at present.

We must support the consecration of women Bishops in the Church of England. This is likely to happen in the next ten years, and it will help to bring about a more inclusive and less patriarchal Church.

The Church of England is now very different from the one I knew when brought up in Shrewsbury over 50 years ago. The 'Stone Age' theology of the Conservative Evangelicals, which my father warned about, has become dominant. At present the future does not look very encouraging. But in another 50 years time Liberal Christianity may again be powerful. Certainly the Church of England will survive, even if the Anglican Communion does not. Liberal Catholicism is already reviving and this is likely to continue.

I shall die long before this story comes to an end. My children may not see much progress. But my prophecy is that Fundamentalism must eventually fade. This will take some time, but intelligent scholarship, education and enlightenment must win in the end. Inclusiveness also for women and gay and lesbian people will come about in Muslim as well as Christian countries. When this happens, future generations will look back at the important role played by the Episcopal Church in the United States of America and the Anglican Church of Canada. They will be seen as the enlightened pioneers who guided by God's Holy Spirit had the courage to change people's attitudes for the better.

Today we admire those who abolished slavery and cannot understand how Christians and Muslims supported it for so long. In another 200 years most Christians and Muslims will not understand why their ancestors did so much harm in the early twenty-first century, but they will admire those who fought and defeated Fundamentalism.

Notes and References

CHAPTER 1 *Anglo-Catholic Childhood*

1 *The Times*, 20th March 2004.
2 Footnote in Bishop Gore's essay *The Holy Spirit and Inspiration* in *Lux Mundi* which he also edited.
3 Steve Chalke *The Last Message of Jesus* (Zonderman Michegan 2003), p.182.
4 Bishop Colin Buchanan *Is the Church of England Biblical?* (Darton Longman & Todd 1998), p.5.
5 Ibid, p5 (footnote).

CHAPTER 2 *A Questioning Education*

1 Harry Thompson *Ingrams* (William Heinemann 1994), p.42.
2 W. H. Auden & Christopher Isherwood *The Ascent of F6* (Faber & Faber 1936).
3 Harry Thompson *Ingrams* (William Heinemann 1994), p.35.
4 Humphrey Carpenter *That Was Satire That Was*(Victor Gollancx & Phoenix 2002), p.36.

CHAPTER 3 *The Army Fosters Ordination*

1 Michael Barber *The Captain: The Life and Times of Simon Raven* (Gerald Duckworth & Co. Ltd 1996), p.127.
2 Ibid, p.127.

CHAPTER 4 *An Intelligent Theology*

1 Herbert Butterfield was Regius Professor of Modern History at Cambridge University. *Christianity & History* was published by Bell in 1949.
2 Dr David Stafford-Clark was physician in charge of the Department of Psychological Medicine and Director of the York Clinic in Guy's Hospital, London (1954–73).
3 John Knox *Criticism and Faith* (Hodder & Stoughton 1953), p.78.
4 J. A. T. Robinson *In the End God . . . A Study of the Christian Doctrine of the Last Things* (James Clarke 1950), p.123.
5 Ibid, pp.122, 123.
6 My summary of Bultmann's theology is based on the following books: *Jesus Christ and Mythology* (SCM Press 1960); *Kerygma and Myth* (Ed. H. W. Bartsch Vols. I & II) (SPCK 1960 and 1962); *Jesus and the Word* (Fontana 1935).

7 My summary of Tillich's theology is based on the following books: *The Shaking of the Foundations* (Pelican); *The New Being* (SCM Press 1955); *The Eternal Now* (SCM Press 1963); *The Courage To Be* (Fontana 1952); *Systematic Theology* Vols. I, II & III (James Nisbet 1960).

8 Joseph Fletcher *Situation Ethics* (SCM Press 1966), p.152.

9 *I Knew Dietrich Bonhoeffer*, edited by Wolf-Dieter Zimmerman & Ronald Gregor Smith (Collins Fontana Books 1973), p.82.

10 *God's Truth*. Essays to celebrate the 25th anniversary of *Honest to God* (SCM Press 1988), p.IX.

CHAPTER 5 *Westminster and Marriage*

1 Keele '67. *The National Evangelical Anglican Congress Statement*, ed. Philip Crowe (1967), p.8; see also the preparatory papers *Guidelines: Anglican Evangelicals Face the Future*, ed. J. I. Packer (1967).

CHAPTER 6 *A South Bank Priest*

1 Ronald Webber *The Peasants Revolt* (Terence Dalton 1980), p.58.

2 *Chanctonbury Ring* (Sheldon Press & Hodder & Stoughton 1982).

3 Trevor Beeson *The Bishops* (SCM Press 2002), p.218.

4 Michael De-la-Noy *Mervyn Stockwood: A Lonely Life* (Mowbray 1996), p.192.

5 Hugh Montefiore *Oh God What Next? An Autobiography* (Hodder & Stoughton 1995), p.145.

CHAPTER 7 *Evangelicals and Theology in the Gutter*

1 Frank Peretti *This Present Darkness* (Crossway Books 1986).

2 Hans Kung *On Being a Christian* (Collins 1978), p.19.

3 John D. Barrow *The Origin of the Universe* (Weidenfled & Nicholson 1994), p.137. He is now Professor of Mathematical Sciences at the University of Cambridge.

4 Cecilia Goodenough *Theology in the Gutter* (not published).

5 Ibid, p.25.

CHAPTER 8 *Faith in the City*

1 *Faith in the City*. The Report of the Archbishop of Canterbury's Commission on Urban Priority Areas (Church House Publishing 1985), pp.xv, xiv.

2 Ibid, p.230.

3 Ibid, p.229.

4 Anne Power *Property Before People: The Management of Twentieth-Century Council Housing* (Allen & Unwin 1987).

5 Report by Walter Schwarz in the *Guardian*, 8th June 1988.

6 David Hare *Asking Around – Background to the David Hare Trilogy* (Faber & Faber, and National Theatre 1993), p.13.

7 Ibid, pp.28, 29.

8 Ibid, p.31. Walter is in fact Richard Moberley.

9 Ibid, p.31, but amended by myself following a telephone call with Richard Moberley.

10 Ibid, pp.41, 13.

11 David Hare *Racing Demon* première in the National Theatre on 8th February 1990.

12 *The Church of England Newspaper* 29th November 1996.

13 *The Times* 26th March 1992. The other signatories were:– John Austin (London), Peter Atkinson (Oxford), Brian Barnes (Canterbury), Richard Freeman (Rochester), Ann Morisy (London), David Partridge (Portsmouth), Chris Rich (Winchester), David Rudd (St Albans), Martin Wallace (Chelmsford).

14 Highlights of: (a) Report in *The Church Times* 31st December 1993; (b) Review in *The Church of England Newspaper* 17th June 1994.

15 *New Woman* December 1990 as printed in *Landmark*, published by Marc Europe, Autumn 1991.

16 European Values Study quoted in the *Independent* 17th September 1991.

17 Andrew N. Wilson *Against Religion* Counterblast 19 (Chatto & Windus 1991).

18 *The Times* 16th April 1997.

19 Report by Kate Watson-Smyth in the *Independent* 5th March 1997.

20 *The Bridge* (newspaper of the Anglican Diocese of Southwark), editorial November 1996.

CHAPTER 9 *Change in the Diocese*

1 *The Times* 9th August 1997.

2 *The Body's Grace*. The Michael Harding Memorial Address by Rowan Williams in 1989, republished by LGCM in 2003.

3 *The Bridge* (newspaper of the Anglican Diocese of Southwark), editorial, November 2003.

4 *The Times* 11th March 1983.

5 *The Bridge* (newspaper of the Anglican Diocese of Southwark), editorial, February 2003.

6 *South London Press* 27th August 1999.

CHAPTER 12 *The Triumph of Fundamentalism*

1 Joan Smith *Religion must be kept in its place*. Article in *The Times* 18th March 2004.

2 Esther Kaplan *With God on their Side* (The New Press, New York & London 2004 & 2005), p3.

3 Gore Vidal *Armageddon?* (Andre Deutsch 1987), p.103.

4 Ibid p.104. Yankelovich Poll 1984.

5 Kenneth Leech *The Sky is Red* (Darton Longman & Todd 1997 & 2003), p.195.

6 Peter Singer *The President of Good and Evil* (Granta Books, London 2004 & Dutton, USA 2004), p.207.

7 Ibid, p.208. Poll in a special issue of *Time* (Fall 1992) *In the New Millennium*.

8 Ibid, p.208. Also Ann McFeatten *Religious Leaders Uneasy with Bush's Rhetoric, Pittsburgh Post-Gazette* 12th February 2003.

9 Ibid, p.208.

10 Ibid, p.208. Also Howard Fineman *Bush & God, Newsweek* 10th March 2003, p.25.

11 Bruce Lincoln *Holy Terrors: Thinking about Religion after September 11th* (University of Chicago Press 2003), p.20.

12 Esther Kaplan *With God on their Side* (The New Press, New York 2005), p.277.

13 Tariq Ali *The Clash of Fundamentalisms* (Verso, New York 2002). Chapter 1 *An Atheist Childhood*.

14 *The Times* 18th March 2004. Article by Joan Smith, *Religion must be kept in its place*.

15 Ibid.

16 Ibid.

17 Tariq Ali *The Clash of Fundamentalisms* (Verso, New York 2002), p.283.

18 Stephen Bates *A Church at War* (I. B. Tauris 2004), p.128.

19 Ibid, p.130.

20 Ibid, p.129.

21 Interview in the *Guardian* 8th September 2003.

22 *The Church Times* 3rd July 2003.

23 *Independent* 29th December 2003.

24 Stephen Bates *A Church at War* (I. B. Taurus 2004), p.192.

25 General Synod of the Church of England, February 2004.

26 Shrewsbury Town Centre Churches. A Report to the Salop Archdeaconry Pastoral Committee by the Bishop of Shrewsbury and the Archdeadon of Salop 1981.

27 *The Salopian* No. 136, June 2005. Article by Peter Fanning.

CHAPTER 13 *Fighting Fundamentalism*

1 You Gov Poll in the *Daily Telegraph* 25th July 2005.

2 Stephen Bates interview with David Banting in September 2003, quoted in *A Church at War* (I. B. Taurus 2004), p23.

3 Stephen Bates *A Church at War* (I. B. Taurus 2004), p.222.

4 *Observer* 19th September 2004 in the Review of Books.

5 *The Times* 18th March 2004, article Religion must be kept in its place.

6 Stephen Bates interview with Bishop Wallace Benn in September 2003, quoted in *A Church at War* (I. B. Taurus 2004), p.16.

7 Ibid, p.20. Stephen Bates interview with Christina Rees.

8 *Guardian* 22nd September 1999. Article *Party for Jesus* by Jonathan Margolis.

9 Stephen Bates interview with David Banting, September 2003, quoted in *A Church at War* (I. B. Taurus 2004), p.22.

10 *The Times* 4th January 2006.

11 Stephen Bates interview with Christina Rees, quoted in *A Church at War* (I. B. Taurus 2004), pp.19,20.

12 ORB Opinion Poll sponsored by the Church of England and carried out by Opinion Research Business Britain in November 2005 and released mid-December 2005.